HANDLE
WITH
PRAYER

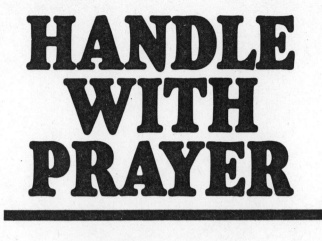

HANDLE WITH PRAYER

Charles F. Stanley

This book is designed for your personal reading pleasure and profit. It is also designed for group study. A leader's guide with helps and hints for teachers and visual aids (Victor Multiuse Transparency Masters) is available from your local bookstore or from the publisher.

VICTOR

BOOKS a division of SP Publications, Inc.
WHEATON. ILLINOIS 60187

Offices also in
Whitby, Ontario, Canada
Amersham-on-the-Hill, Bucks, England

Third printing, 1983

Dr. Stanley is also the author of one other book from Victor: *A Man's Touch*

Most of the Scripture quotations in this book are from the *King James Version*. Other quotations are from the *New American Standard Bible* (NASB), © 1960, 1962, 1963, 1968, 1971, 1972, 1973 by the Lockman Foundation, La Habra, California. Used by permission.

Recommended Dewey Decimal Classification: 248.3
  Suggested Subject Headings: PRAYER; PRIVATE WORSHIP

Library of Congress Catalog Card Number: 81-86291
ISBN: 0-88207-309-5

VICTOR BOOKS
A division of SP Publications, Inc.
P. O. Box 1825 ● Wheaton, Illinois 60187

Contents

To my mother
Rebecca,
who taught me to pray.

1
Unveiling the Hidden

Moreover the word of the Lord came unto Jeremiah the second time, while he was yet shut up in the court of the prison, saying, "Thus saith the Lord the Maker thereof, the Lord that formed it, to establish it; the Lord is His name; 'Call unto Me, and I will answer thee, and show thee great and mighty things, which thou knowest not.' "

Jeremiah 33:1-3

As I was praying one afternoon in 1967, I began feeling as if God had something very specific to say to me. The more I prayed, the more the burden increased. I mentioned this to my wife, and we decided to take our vacation early and spend the time seeking God's guidance. We went to the mountains of North Carolina for two weeks, intent on finding out what God was saying to me.

Annie and I spent the majority of our time fasting and praying. We waited, expecting God to follow up the burden with an answer. To our surprise, He pointed out areas in our lives that needed correcting. The entire two weeks was a period of personal cleansing and preparation for what was to come.

We went back home excited, but still unsure. Things were better for us personally, but it was as if there was a veil that kept me from knowing the unknown. I felt that the answer was close, but it was still out of my grasp. Then one afternoon soon afterward, I was on my face before the Lord and the veil lifted. God wanted me to start a school. I hesitated to commit myself to such a task, but God made it clear to me that His instructions were to be *obeyed*, not just considered. He unveiled the hidden to me when I called on Him to do so; He showed me the things I knew not of. God was faithful, even to the point of preparing my heart for what He had to say.

God desires to make known the unknown to His children. He desires to unveil the hidden. Yet many times we are satisfied not knowing. Either we aren't willing to take the time to wait, or we aren't sure God even wants us to know. But this command to Jeremiah speaks specifically to both of these problems. We are to call, we are to expect an answer, and we are to know the unknown. Let's look at the background of this Scripture in Jeremiah (33:1-3).

The Babylonians are coming toward Jerusalem from the east. They have already defeated the Assyrians, so the people of Jerusalem know they don't stand much of a chance against their superior military strength. The leaders of Jerusalem believed they should align themselves with the Egyptians, which was the logical thing to do. But Jeremiah tells them, "God says you are going into captivity. What you really ought to do is go out there and surrender." Well, this wasn't at all what the leaders had in mind. They threw Jeremiah in prison and refused to listen to him.

We should not be surprised at their reaction. What do you think the people in my congregation would do if I stood up next Sunday and said, "God says the Russians are going to overthrow this nation. We might as well surrender now and save ourselves some trouble"? They would run me out of town! But this was exactly the situation Jeremiah found himself in. From his experience he gives us a passage (33:1-3) that helps us understand how to talk with God.

Encouraged to Pray

There are three things in this verse we need to understand. The first is that God encourages us to pray, "Call unto Me." Since Jeremiah was in prison, he had a long time to catch up on his prayer life. We may never be put behind bars, but God will put us in circumstances and situations in order to teach us how to talk with Him.

Most of the time we pray "Get me out of here!" We want to avoid suffering and difficulty. When we *do* run into a trial or difficulty, we ask God to change our circumstances so we can serve Him better and love Him more.

But we cannot fool God or bribe Him with our promises. Jeremiah didn't even ask God to get him out of prison. Rather, he waited to see what God would say to him. And what did God reply? "Call unto Me and I will answer thee and show thee great and mighty things which thou knowest not" (33:3). What God did for Jeremiah had a far greater impact than simply getting him out of prison.

But most of us aren't that patient. We're more intent on getting out of our circumstances than we are on finding out what great things God wants to show us. But God never allows difficulty just for the sake of difficulty—there is always a higher purpose involved. The problem is we cannot always identify God's higher purpose in the midst of our trials. That's when we must exercise our faith by waiting on His Word for us.

A good friend of mine, who was a real estate broker, experienced a seven year period of financial failure. The loss of his security devastated him. It became the constant focus of his thoughts and prayers. "Why doesn't God do something?" he would ask me. For a while it was a mystery to both of us.

But after some intense soul searching, he realized that he had substituted financial security for God in his life. God wanted to be recognized as the Source of all things in my friend's life. As he began renewing his mind spiritually and yielding his rights to the Lord, he gained a new freedom in his attitude toward finances. He started a new career and found greater financial blessing than ever before.

God had a great and mighty lesson to teach my friend; a lesson more important than keeping him comfortable. And God kept him uncomfortable till he took his eyes off his circumstances and sought God's mind in the matter.

Waiting is not easy. Often we turn away from seeking God's counsel and seek guidance from friends and loved ones. We read books, attend seminars, and talk with others trying to find out what God has to say to us. Usually after we've exhausted all other possibilities, we turn back to the Lord and wait on Him. By doing this we are saying to God, "Now that I've tried everything else and failed, I've decided I need You after all."

But God wants us to come to Him first. He wants us to stand in His counsel and wait for His Word. He longs for us to come to Him as a son would to his father. But instead we go to Him last, as if we don't trust Him or consider His Word of much value. Yet, He is the only trustworthy Source of counsel we have; He is our most available and accessible Friend. He will never give us a busy signal. But He frequently gets busy signals when He tries talking to us.

God entreats us to pray because He knows we are often caught in prisons of our own making. Not prisons with bars and locks, but intellectual prisons, emotional prisons, and relational prisons. Remember, the shortest distance between a problem and the solution is the distance between our knees and the floor.

Answer Promised

Secondly, God told Jeremiah, "I will answer thee." Sometimes we make commitments that we cannot keep. We may do it unintentionally, but nevertheless at times we disappoint those who are counting on us. But when God Almighty says He will do something, it will be done.

God says He will not only hear, but will answer our prayers. This brings us to an interesting question. Does God always answer our prayers? Or does He only respond to certain kinds of prayer? Think about the requests you have made of God recently. Are they being answered? Do you really believe they will be? You see, the question is not *Does God answer prayer?* The real question is *How does God answer prayer?* Sometimes He answers *yes*. This is usually the only answer we hear. If God says *yes* then we believe He answered. If He says *no*, we think He ignored our request.

God's Answers

When God answers our prayers, He either answers with yes, no, or wait. When He answers yes, we are prone to shout, "Praise the Lord!" We tell everybody what a great thing God has done for us.

But when God says no, we have a hard time finding reasons to praise Him. We look for the sin in our lives that kept Him from granting our requests, because surely if we had been living right He would have answered yes. But not one shred of scriptural evidence shows that God will say yes to all our prayers just because we're living right. God is sovereign. He has the right to say no according to His infinite wisdom, regardless of our goodness.

We try to manipulate God by our humanistic "if then" philosophy. *If* we live good clean lives, *then* God must (we believe) grant our hearts' desires. But such attempts to manipulate God defeat the whole purpose of Christianity, which is to glorify Him through our submissive obedience to His desires. And besides, if our goodness was the only factor God considered, where would His grace fit in? As it is, many times His grace is what motivates Him to say no.

God only says *no* and *wait* when it is best for us (Rom. 8:28). He does it many times for our protection. Sometimes God *wants* to answer our prayer, but the timing is not right. For example, many couples wanting to get married come to me for counseling. Sometimes I advise them to wait. Some take my advice, while others seek counsel from those who tell them what they want to hear. You and I have the same choice over and over again. Will we wait on God for His perfect timing, or will we rush ahead?

We don't like waiting around, especially when it looks like a unique opportunity might slip away. We don't like to hear God say *no*, especially when everything in us says *yes, yes, yes*! Often we try to find a Scripture verse and claim it while we continue our prayer, hoping somehow to change God's mind. What we're really saying is, "God, I didn't like that answer. How about reconsidering my point of view?"

But deep in our hearts we really want God's perfect will for our lives. And we must remember that God's answer is always His ultimate best for us. Claiming Scripture will not change God's mind because His Word cannot contradict His will. If He says no, then the answer is no. If He says wait, then we should wait. God is more interested in our character, our future, and our sanctification than He is in our momentary satisfaction. His answers are always an act of grace, motivated by His love.

Our Response

Our response to God's answers reveals one of two things about us. It will reveal either a rebellious spirit or a submissive spirit. By accepting God's answer, despite the fact that we may not understand, we express a submissive spirit. But by refusing His first answer and trying to get our way by manipulation, we express a rebellious spirit.

If we refuse God's answers when they don't fit in with our plans, then we are trying to use God for our purposes. But if we graciously accept His answers no matter what they are, He will use us for His glory.

The Hidden Revealed

The third thing this verse says is, "I will show thee great and mighty things which thou knowest not." All of us face decisions that leave us baffled. We are constantly bombarded with marital decisions, business decisions, household decisions, and financial decisions—and they all need immediate attention. In this verse, God promises to reveal the answer to all life's decisions. Yet many of God's people spend their entire lives making decisions based on *their* knowledge, *their* understanding, and *their* experience—not realizing that some decisions must be based on divine wisdom and illumination from God.

Almost any preacher can prepare a sermon. He can write an outline, gather a few stories, and away he goes. But a preacher cannot get God's message for a people till he waits in His counsel, till he seeks God's face, and till God gives him a Word from heaven (Jer. 23:21-22).

This same principle applies to every Christian. We can pay the price required to find God's mind on an issue, or we can make a decision based on what *we* think is right. Either way, a decision will eventually be made. But while one decision may have the approval of man, the other will have the eternal approval of God.

Sometimes we flip a coin, spiritually speaking, and say, "Lord, this is what I'm going to do. If it is of You, then bless it. If I'm wrong, then better luck next time." Instead of waiting, we jump ahead and hope we have done the right thing. The point is this, as Christians we never have to guess—we can know for sure. God wants us to know His will about things even more than we want to know it. But He cannot, and will not, bless anything we do that is not of Him.

So what does He mean when He says, "I will show thee great and mighty things"? Every time we pray to God, seeking His will, there are two things He wants to show us. He wants to show us Himself (Phil. 3:7-8), and He wants to show us what He is able to do (John 15:16). Is there anything greater than seeking God and knowing His power?

We Are to Seek His Face
Because God wants first to show us His face, and because our goal as Christians is to know Him, we should begin our time in prayer by saying something like this: "Lord, thank You that You are omnipotent. Thank You that You are omniscient, and know everything I am about to tell You. Thank You that

You are omnipresent, and You are not separated from me. As I come into Your presence, I bow my heart and my body before Your throne to thank You for Your holiness, Your forgiveness, and Your mercy. I acknowledge You as the great Creator, the great Sustainer, the great Lover of mankind. Father, I am coming to You, recognizing Your greatness, and Your holiness. I bow before You as Your child, knowing that You are more than sufficient to meet my needs."

That is the spirit in which we should come into God's presence. But instead we come first with our needs and usually don't have enough time for anything else. We never stop long enough to recognize that God wants to show us Himself when we pray.

He Shows Us His Power

The second great thing He wants to show us is what He is able and willing to do. He does this through His Word. He reminds us of what He has done in the past. He gives us example after example in Scripture of how He met people's needs and protected them. And He is willing to do the same thing for us if we will only ask.

The word "mighty" in this passage means hidden things, things that are fenced in. This word is used when referring to fortified cities. God is saying that as we pray, He will unveil insights for us that have previously been a mystery.

This also implies that some answers will only be found in prayer, not from other sources—not from books, not from friends, and not from counselors. Some things must come straight from God, the Source of all wisdom. How many families would still be together today if they had sought God's answers to their problems at home? How many sons and daughters would still be home if their parents had taken their situation to the Lord? But often we refuse to wait on God's answers. We want quick solutions to our problems.

But God wants to do much more than just meet our needs and answer our questions. He wants our love. He wants our spirits. He wants our lives. Yes, He encourages us to bring our trials and our heartaches to Him in prayer, but only after we recognize who He is and what He can do. Only then do we believe He will answer our prayers. Only then are we seeking His face, and not merely His hand.

As a pastor, many times I go to God for answers that can be found only in Him. Sometimes He shows me something for today and sometimes He shows me something that will happen the next week or the next month. But I've never been to God about anything He did not willingly answer. He does not always answer my prayers according to *my* time schedule, but He is always on time.

Back in 1969 while I was preaching a week long revival meeting in Virginia, I felt once again that God had something specific to say to me. Each night after the service I retired to my room early to pray. One night I pulled out a pad and drew a circle with five lines leading from it. At the end of each line, I wrote one of several things I thought God may be trying to say to me. On the last line I drew a question mark, thinking maybe it was something I had not thought of.

The following night I came back to my room with the same burden. As I prayed and looked over the possibilities, God made it clear that He was going to move me. I asked Him when, and the month of September flashed into my mind. This happened in May of 1969, but I thought that He meant September 1970. A few months later, however, a pulpit committee from The First Baptist Church of Atlanta came to see me. On September 30, 1969 my family and I moved to Atlanta. God told me ahead of time in order to prepare my heart. He unveiled the hidden when I called on Him to do so.

Regardless of what circumstances you are up against, there is no knowledge you will ever need that is not accessible before the throne of our living, loving, holy, righteous God. He has promised to show you the great, the hidden, and the unknown things that you will never be able to understand any other way. There are some things you will never be able to know (Deut. 29:29), but all the knowledge you will ever need is available if you ask God.

God desires to illuminate your mind and heart till you are conscious of Christ's mind within you. He wants you to say no to the world on the basis of your faith in Him. It is then that you feel an extra sense of power when you share with others. You no longer depend entirely on circumstances for God to teach you lessons. Instead you learn straight from Him through His Word. You have a new excitement in your relationship with God, because you have learned to listen as He speaks to you.

Submission Required

You must be submissive to Him to the point of absolute obedience regardless of what He asks. Why? Because if God continues to answer our prayers and we have certain conditions on which we obey, then He is nothing more than a giant Santa Claus. If He continued to bless us regardless of our rebellion, we would be using Him for our ends, not His. Submission is essential.

If you have been seeking God's will for a long time and you seem to be getting nowhere, examine your heart. See if there is any area of your life that is not totally surrendered to God. By settling this issue, you will put yourself in a position that will allow God to bless you. The quicker you move from your will to His will, the quicker God will show you what you need to know. Since God gives us His Word for obedience, not just consideration, He must be assured that you have submitted yourself completely before He will let you in on His secrets.

Are you facing a decision in your life that is too big for you to handle? Are you going through some difficulty that has left you confused and disheartened? God said, "Call unto Me and I will answer thee and show thee great and mighty things which thou knowest not." As you seek God's face and understand who He is and what He is willing and able to do, He will clear away all the mist that surrounds your circumstances. He will show you what to do. Are you willing to say yes to whatever He requires? If so, you have taken the first step in learning to talk with God.

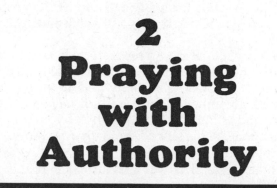

2
Praying with Authority

And it came to pass at the time of the offering of the evening sacrifice, that Elijah the prophet came near, and said, "Lord God of Abraham, Isaac, and of Israel, let it be known this day that Thou art God in Israel, and that I am Thy servant, and that I have done all these things at Thy word. Hear me, O Lord, hear me, that this people may know that Thou art the Lord God, and that Thou hast turned their heart back again." Then the fire of the Lord fell, and consumed the burnt sacrifice, and the wood, and the stones, and the dust, and licked up the water that was in the trench. And when all the people saw it, they fell on their faces: and they said, "The Lord, He is the God; the Lord, He is the God."

1 Kings 18:36-39

Ahab and Elijah had been enemies for a long time. So Elijah challenged Ahab and the prophets of Baal to a contest. He said, "Let's find out whose god is really God. If the god of Baal is God, we should all worship him. If Jehovah is God, then we should all follow Him."

Ahab thought this was fair enough and agreed to go along

with Elijah's plan. Elijah instructed him to build an altar and find a suitable sacrifice for his god. Then all the prophets of Baal were to pray and ask their god to consume the offering with fire.

Well, the prophets of Baal prepared their altar and began to pray. They not only prayed, but they shouted and cried and cut themselves trying to get their god to prove himself. Finally, Elijah got annoyed, and started ridiculing them. He teased them and asked, "What's wrong? Is your god asleep? Is he on vacation?" This stirred them up even more, but still nothing happened.

Then Elijah decided it was his turn. He rebuilt an old forgotten altar of God and placed his sacrifice on it. Then to prove his point, he had a barrel of water poured over it. This was repeated twice, till everything was drenched. Satisfied with the altar and sacrifice, Elijah prayed. While everyone watched and listened, Elijah asked God to prove to the whole host that He was the God of Israel. Not only did God consume the sacrifice with fire, but also the wood, the stones, the dust, and the water as well (1 Kings 18:38). The Lord God had proven Himself.

This is a beautiful demonstration of praying with authority. Elijah didn't hide out in some quiet place and have a prayer meeting and then tell everyone that God had answered his prayer. If he had, no one would have believed him, and God would not have had the opportunity to prove Himself to the people.

But when Elijah built an altar before all the prophets of Baal, and soaked it with water, he put himself in a do-or-die situation. Either God had to come through, or Elijah would be accused of serving a dead god. So with a sense of humility and desperation, Elijah cried to God and God answered with fire from heaven. There was not anything private about Elijah's faith. As a result, God demonstrated His supernatural power publicly. Elijah saw a dream come true when the people said, "The Lord, He is the God." Elijah knew then that he had accomplished his purpose.

Another Example

A few years ago, a certain international missionary organization was having a week long conference for all their
missionaries. This would be the last time many of these
missionaries would be able to leave their countries because of
the anti-religious stand by their governments.

One missionary from Burma, Ouan Lei, had tried for
almost a year to get permission to leave that country. But time
after time his application for a visa was rejected. On the first
night of the conference, after all the preliminary introduc-
tions were taken care of, one missionary from the United
States stood and said he believed that God wanted their
friend from Burma to be at that conference.

No one said a word as this older saint began to pray. He
began by binding Satan. Then he asked that God change the
minds of the officials who were in charge of issuing the visas.
He prayed for about 20 minutes and sat down. After a few
more minutes of silence, the conference was resumed.

About an hour and a half later, a woman from the kitchen
came running into the room to announce that someone had
just called from Burma and that Ouan Lei had just received
permission to leave the country. Like Elijah, that saint from
the United States knew how to pray with the kind of authority
that moves God.

Claiming God's Promises

Think of all the promises God has given in the Scriptures
about answered prayer. How many do we claim on a daily
basis? Instead we complain about our needs and our
problems. We tiptoe around in the throne room of God,
afraid to ask what we really want. We don't go to Him on the
basis of what He said He would do. We go weakly and
fearfully.

But according to Scripture we are to go boldly (Heb. 4:16).
When we leave our place of prayer, we should be expecting
God's answer. God doesn't want us walking around with
attitudes of fear and doubt, wondering if He will do anything

about our requests. He has given us a spirit of power, not one of timidity (2 Tim. 1:7).

"For we have not an high priest which cannot be touched with the feeling of our infirmities; but was in all points tempted like as we are, yet without sin. Let us therefore come boldly unto the throne of grace, that we may obtain mercy, and find grace to help in time of need" (Heb. 4:15-16). Christ is our go-between to God. We get to God on the basis of Christ's righteousness, not our own. Therefore, we can go to God the Father with the same authority that Christ did. This is the reason we can go to God boldly and with a sense of authority. Because of our position in Christ we can pray with authority, believing that God will honor our prayers.

Jehoshaphat's Example

Let's look at another good example of praying with authority. Jehoshaphat had just heard the news that a great multitude was coming against him from beyond the seas to take the people of God into captivity. Scripture says Jehoshaphat was afraid and called for fasting and prayer throughout the nation. In desperation and fear, he cried out to the Lord. In essence he prayed, "O God of heaven, is it not You who is Master over all the nations in the earth? We have no might. We have no strength. All we can do is focus our attention on You." (See 2 Chron. 20:6-12.) God heard Jehoshaphat's prayer and caused their enemies to destroy themselves.

Elijah and Jehoshaphat are two clear examples of men who approached God fearlessly, boldly, and courageously, making petitions that would allow God to glorify Himself. But how often do we go to God concentrating on our own sense of inability and helplessness? We say, "Oh Lord, You know my needs. I hope You will do something about them." That is not praying with authority, but with defeat.

God's Power and Authority in Us

Praying with authority doesn't mean we go to God proudly, demanding our way in spite of His will. The concept of authority means something entirely different. Christ said,

"All power is given unto Me in heaven and in earth" (Matt. 28:18). The Greek word used here for power (*exousia*) means that Christ had the power and freedom to do anything He pleased with no hindrances. He had unlimited power and unlimited freedom to use it.

"But ye shall receive power, after that the Holy Ghost is come upon you" (Acts 1:8). The word used in this verse comes from a different Greek word (*dynamis*). It means having the supernatural capacity of God to bring forth something in the name of Jesus Christ. Christ had God's power in an unlimited capacity, whereas we have God's power in conjunction with accomplishing His will. So when Christ sent the disciples out (Matt. 28), they went with the confidence that they would be granted all the power they needed. Since Christ had all the power in heaven and earth, He could give them that same power.

Both types of power are mentioned in Luke 9:1. "Then He called His twelve disciples together and gave them power [*dynamis*] and authority [*exousia*] over all devils, and to cure diseases." He gave them the divine capacity to execute the will of God. At this point in their ministry, they received the ability to bring forth what God had commissioned them to do. But having the ability was not enough. They had to have the authority, or the right to claim their position of power over all demons and illnesses; Christ gave them that right.

When God gives us a commission, He always equips us for the job. God has made provision for our needs before the needs ever arise. Our problem is that we don't apply the power and authority He has made available to us. As a result, we come up answerless and frustrated in our prayer lives. This will continue till we do God's work in God's power, not our own.

God has placed in the hands of every believer the most miraculous and supernatural power this world will ever know. Yet we still live powerless lives, pray powerless prayers, and do powerless works. As a result, the church is weak. And because the church is weak, the nation is weak. We will never accomplish what God wants accomplished as a body, or as individuals, till we learn to go to Him claiming the power and authority He has granted us; a power and authority that gives us the right and ability to do the works of God.

This authority does not give us license to make demands of God. By studying the prayers of Elijah and Jehoshaphat, we see that they went to God with a deep sense of humility. They went with boldness, but not with pride. Humility is essential if we desire to pray with authority. Humility means agreeing with God about who we are and what we can do. Humility eliminates the idea that we tell God what to do. In actuality, we are crying out in desperation for Him to intervene in our circumstances.

Praying with authority is essential if we are to pray effective prayers that free God to work. Praying without authority lacks urgency, which allows Satan to sidetrack us. Without urgency we lose heart in our prayers. The least little thing becomes an excuse to quit. Without a sense of urgency, our minds are easily divided. How many times have you found yourself saying empty heartless words that you felt got no higher than the ceiling? Lack of urgency in prayer gives Satan the foothold he needs to completely demoralize and despiritualize our prayer life.

Prayer—Our Spiritual Battlefield

Why does Satan put such a high priority on destroying our prayer life? Paul wrote, "For we wrestle not against flesh and blood, but against principalities, against powers, against the rulers of the darkness of this world, against spiritual wickedness in high places" (Eph. 6:12). As Christians we are in a spiritual battle. The only time Satan worries about us is when we enter into this battle. Nothing else we do is much of a threat. Satan knows that real spiritual battle is done on our knees. Prayer is the weapon he fears most; therefore it is prayer against which he makes his greatest attack. It is on our knees that the greatest good is done, and it is on our knees that we will face the greatest assaults.

There was a period in my life when every time I knelt to pray I would fall asleep. Regardless of how much sleep I had, I could not stay awake when I began to pray. I did everything I knew to do, but nothing helped. I had no problem studying, even when I arose early, but I couldn't pray 10 minutes without falling asleep.

I struggled with this for almost a year till the Lord revealed the problem to me. Satan would rather I preach or study than pray. He would rather I do *anything* than pray. To hinder me, he attacked me with a spirit of slumber. When I realized this, I asked God to tear down this stronghold of slumber and replace it with a spirit of alertness. The problem immediately disappeared. The joy of my prayer life was revived, the struggle with slumber ceased, and once again I entered into the heat of the battle.

Paul tells the believer how to prepare for this spiritual battle (Eph. 6:13-17). He makes it clear that *all* the armor is essential if we are to stand firm. Paul knew that prayer was much more than rushing to God and making a few quick requests. He saw it as a battle and we must see it that way too. It is in prayer that battles are won and lost. Therefore, it is essential that we learn to pray.

Satan not only attacks our concentration in prayer, but our faith as well. As long as we pray with no authority, doubts can slip in. He will do everything in his power to increase our doubts and destroy our faith.

Satan uses these doubts against us by saying things like, "You can't ask God for that. Who do you think you are? You are just a sinner. What makes you think you can bother a holy God with your little problems?"

The problem is that without any authority in our prayers, we cannot rebuke him and bind him from our thoughts. In the same way, the church is powerless against Satan's attacks unless it gets the power and authority of God back into its prayers. Satan would love for the church to continue the way it has in past generations, coming timidly to the gates of hell with no prevailing power whatsoever. But this is our own fault. We attempt to fight this battle in the flesh, not in the spirit. We're fighting a spiritual battle without spiritual power, and we're losing.

Satan is not concerned with how many times we go to church or how many hymns we sing. He does not feel threatened by our organizations or our machinery. But when God's people fall on their knees and claim Christ's power and authority, everything in heaven will begin to move, and everything in hell will begin to shake.

Our Relationship

There are five prerequisites if we are to go to God with a sense of authority. First we must have a genuine personal relationship with God through His Son Jesus Christ. Since our authority is based on our position in Christ, we must be in Him to receive His authority. Salvation is the first step.

God's Thoughts

Secondly we must know God's thoughts (1 Cor. 2:11-12). This is one of the main reasons God has given us the Scriptures. The Bible shows us God's thoughts in our vocabulary. The more we saturate our minds with Scripture, the more like God we will think. His view of things will become our view. His attitudes will become our attitudes.

As a result it becomes easier for us to know His will, and knowing His will is essential if we are to pray with authority. Why? Because if we know we are praying in agreement with God about something, we also know it is just a matter of time till He will bring it about. Knowing His will in our prayers gives us the confidence that He is on our side.

Sometimes we run into questions that don't seem to be answered in Scripture. Some circumstances and problems seem so unique that we may not even look to Scripture for an answer. We feel the need to go to another source. But there are no unique problems. Somewhere, somebody has run into a similar situation, or one where the same principles are involved. In Scripture God has provided us with basic principles for handling any circumstance we face. But it is up to us to search the Scriptures to find out what His Word says.

Another way God speaks to us is through the prayers of biblical characters. Find a prayer that goes along with your particular problem or need, and put the prayer in your own words. Then see how God answered that prayer in the life of the one who prayed it. It may be a prayer for wisdom as Solomon prayed, or a cry for help as in Jehoshaphat's case. But remember that the same God who met the needs of those men is able to meet your needs too.

The key is to pray according to God's will. To know His will we must know His thoughts. To know His thoughts we must saturate our minds with His Word. Then we will begin to experience the authority of God in our prayers.

Pure Heart

Thirdly we must have pure hearts if we are to pray with authority. There can be no known sin in our lives. Sin means a divided loyalty. God will not trust His authority and power to anyone who is not completely yielded to His purpose. But when we *do* sin, we must confess and repent. Not just so we can get God's power back, but out of a genuine spirit of sorrow and grief over our sin.

One afternoon a woman and her husband came to see me for marriage counseling. As they described their problems, it became evident that the wife was suffering from satanic oppression. I told them what I thought their problem was and asked for permission to pray for the wife's deliverance and protection. They both quickly agreed and so we prayed.

Three days later the husband called and told me things were worse than before. There seemed to be no change in his wife and they were both discouraged. This troubled me greatly. *Why didn't God answer my prayer?* I thought. As I began to meditate on Scripture, God brought to my mind an area of disobedience that I had not dealt with. I realized that this sin had negated my power and authority to bind Satan from that woman's life. I made things right with the Lord and called the couple back to set up another counseling session. When they came, we prayed again. This time a miraculous change took place. The woman's erratic behavior stopped immediately, her oppression lifted, her countenance changed, and her fellowship with her husband was restored. But it wasn't until I dealt with my own life that God was free to work in hers.

Often Satan will try to use sin against us when we pray. This is why we shouldn't dwell on our sins once they have been confessed. Satan wants us walking around feeling guilty and unworthy. But it is the righteousness of Christ that allows us entry to the Father. It is a righteousness which comes from God on the basis of faith (Phil. 3:9). So once sin has been properly dealt with, we should forget it.

Pure Motives

Fourthly we need pure motives if we are to pray with authority. Remember what Elijah said? "Lord, you know why I did this. I am Your servant and I have done all these things at Your word." When we go to the heavenly Father, we must know in our hearts that our motives are pure. We must pray according to God's will, not according to our own selfish desires clothed in inappropriate Scripture.

However, not *every* personal request is selfish. The key is to have committed our lives to God before we start praying. That way we will want God's will more than the particular thing for which we are asking. When God knows we want His purpose accomplished more than we want anything else, He can trust us with His power. But as long as we pray with selfish motives, we cannot be trusted.

A Persistent Confidence

Fifthly we must have a persistent confidence in the faithfulness of God. This means that the consistency of His Word will be reflected in the consistency of our prayers. We must pray till we see an answer. If we really believe we are praying according to God's will, then why should we stop praying before we see an answer? Many times we pray fervently for a while, then we lose interest and say, "Well, I guess it wasn't God's will." This is an excuse for our lack of importunity. But if we are to pray with authority, we must continue in the battle till we see victory.

Praying with authority is a basic truth that must be applied if we are to learn to talk with God effectively. It is a matter of claiming that which has already been bought and paid for by Christ at Calvary. When we pray with the authority God gave us, we will see our prayers become the effective tools they were meant to be. Our lives and the lives of those around us will be changed. His authority has been promised. Now we must decide whether or not to pay the price necessary to make it a part of our lives.

3
Praying
and
Fasting

Take heed that ye do not your alms before men, to
be seen by them; otherwise ye have no reward of
your Father, who is in heaven. . . . And when thou
prayest, thou shalt not be as the hypocrites are; for
they love to pray standing in the synagogues and in
the corners of the streets, that they may be seen by
men. Verily I say unto you, they have their reward.
. . . Moreover, when ye fast, be not, as the
hypocrites, of a sad countenance; for they disfigure
their faces, that they may appear unto men to fast.
Verily I say unto you, they have their reward. But
thou, when thou fastest, anoint thine head, and
wash thy face, that thou appear not unto men to fast,
but unto thy Father, who is in secret; and thy Father,
who seeth in secret, shall reward thee openly.

Matthew 6:1, 5, 16-18

At the start of my third year of seminary, the pulpit
committee of a little church in North Carolina extended a call
to me to be their pastor. I was also offered a teaching postion
at a Bible Institute near the church. The church would allow
me to teach in the Institute while serving as pastor.

But I had never been a pastor. While my feelings were mixed, the overwhelming emotions were fear and inadequacy. As my wife and I prayed and talked about the opportunity, my list of negatives grew every day. The congregation would have to wait seven months for me, and by then they may have found someone else they liked better.

I was totally ignorant of the real problems facing a pastor. Besides, I felt that the pastors who studied at the Bible Institute wouldn't listen to an inexperienced seminary graduate teach them homiletics (sermon preparation), preaching (sermon delivery), and evangelism.

Back and forth I went: "No, it can't be God's will." "Yes, it must be of Him—I didn't ask for this." For several weeks my faith wavered. I was growing mentally, emotionally, and physically weary. I couldn't get clear direction from the Lord.

Then one morning I was reading from the Book of Daniel. As I began chapter nine, hope swelled within me. I knew I had found a way to know God's will and to know for sure. If God honored Daniel's fasting, why wouldn't He honor mine?

I had never fasted before. As I look back, I realize that I had never felt the need. But I was desperate then for God's clear direction.

After three days of fasting, confessing, listening, and searching the Word, I felt clean, pruned, filled, and confident that the call was God's assignment. I would go with the assurance of His divine assistance.

In June of the following year we moved to Fruitland, North Carolina to an exciting ministry that will always be a highlight of my life. For it was the call to that ministry which revealed my need to practice the biblical principles of fasting.

History

Throughout history a new thirst for God has always awakened a renewed interest in fasting. It was true of Old Testament saints such as Moses the lawgiver, David the King, Elijah the prophet, and Daniel the seer.

Reformers such as John Calvin, Martin Luther, and John

Knox practiced fasting. So did revivalists like Jonathan Edwards, John Wesley, and Charles G. Finney.

There are evidences today that a new thirst for the Spirit is once again beginning to awaken the slumbering church. And once again there is a growing interest in the practice of fasting.

Fasting Defined

First, let's define the term *fasting*. It is more than mere self-denial or abstinence, but it does involve both. It is abstinence with a spiritual goal in mind. Fasting is abstinence from anything that hinders our communion with God.

According to Scripture, fasting can take several forms. First there is the food fast, which means abstaining from all food, illustrated by Christ's fast following His baptism (Luke 4:2). Second is the absolute fast, which means abstaining from drinking as well as eating. This is illustrated by Ezra's fast as he mourned over the faithlessness of the people of God in Exile (Ezra 10:6). A third form of fasting involves the mutual consent of marriage partners to abstain from sexual relations. This is the implication of Paul's exhortation to the married (1 Cor. 7:3-6).

In Matthew 6, Christ talks about praying, giving, and fasting (vv. 1-18). He stresses that we check our motives. We must ask ourselves, *Why am I doing this*? We are not to do these things to be seen by others. We are to pray in secret, not in public like the hypocrites. We are to give in such a way that no one knows how much we give. And when we fast, it should be kept between us and the Lord.

Prayer, giving, and fasting are private acts of worship, and therefore should be done privately. We should do them out of love for God, not because we crave the world's praise. If we do these things for the praise of the world, then that is all the blessing we will receive.

Christ did not say that our witness should be kept to ourselves, but rather certain forms of worship—in this case prayer, fasting, and giving. This will keep us from becoming proud and comparing ourselves with other Christians.

Throughout Scripture, references are made to fasting as an aid to prayer. Before Moses received the Ten Commandments he fasted and prayed (Ex. 34:28). David fasted to deepen his own relationship with the Father (Ps. 69:10). Often when the nation of Israel was being attacked, the leaders called the people to fast and pray, asking God to intervene on their behalf (2 Chron. 20:3). Daniel spent a prolonged period fasting and praying to discern God's timetable concerning Israel's return to Jerusalem from Babylonian captivity (Dan. 9:3). After hearing God's warning through Jonah, the nation of Nineveh began to fast and pray, and God withheld His judgment (Jonah 3:5).

Jesus spent the first 40 days after His baptism fasting and praying, seeking the mind of His Father (Luke 4:1-2). When the New Testament church began, the believers fasted and prayed. Before Paul and Barnabas were sent out, they fasted and prayed (Acts 13:2-3).

Throughout the Bible God directed His people to fast and pray. And every time people fasted and prayed, God released His supernatural power to bring about whatever was necessary to meet their needs. Whether it was wisdom or the defeat of an enemy, God was always faithful to provide.

Since God so mightily honored the prayers of Bible men and women who fasted, we should make fasting a part of our lives as well. But there are four principles we must understand if we are going to effectively combine the tool of fasting with our prayers.

Obedience

First of all, fasting does not negate our responsibility to be obedient to God. We cannot fast and pray expecting God to bless when there is known sin in our lives. Fasting does not impress God with our spirituality to the point that He ignores our sin. On the contrary, genuine fasting will always cause us to examine our hearts to make sure everything is right with Him.

If God exposes some sin in our lives while we're fasting, we must deal with it in whatever manner He requires. This may mean an interruption in our prayertime while we make things right with someone we have offended, or it may mean a commitment to make restitution at a later date. The point is that fasting may be used by God to *expose* sin, but it cannot be used by us to *cover up* sin.

The Control of Appetites

The second principle is that fasting brings our physical appetites under the Holy Spirit's control. We all have appetites or drives. There is the hunger drive, the sex drive, emotional drives, approval drive, and many more. God has given us these drives to be fulfilled within the boundaries of His Word. There are times, however, when we are to set aside the fulfilling of these drives so that we may seek Him with our whole hearts. As we do this, we reach the point that our greatest desire will be undisturbed communion with the Father. We are able to talk with Him more honestly and listen more attentively.

These appetites and drives are not evil, though they are often thought to be. They are gifts from God. But if abused, they can become curses. This is why they must be kept in subjection to our desire for God. Our drives were given in order that they may serve us. But when they get out of balance, we become their slaves. By fasting, we can restore the balance God originally intended.

As a pastor, I counsel many people who are slaves to their drives. The most common problem is in the area of sexual lust. "I'm trapped. I can't help myself. Please help me. I'm afraid of what I might do." These are the cries of sincere believers caught in the web of a desire out of control—lust.

Often it requires more than reading the Bible to be freed from such bondage. Thought patterns must be changed. The mind must be renewed (Rom. 12:1-2). The sex drive has to be brought under the authority of the Holy Spirit. Fasting is a divine aid in bringing about this change.

One afternoon a young man came into my office weeping. He told me about his long and futile battle against lust. He had tried everything he knew to get victory, but nothing worked.

As we talked, I challenged him to fast for three days. I told him to seclude himself and spend his time in two activities. First he was to pray—not, "Oh Lord, please help me," but rather praising God and thanking Him for the victory he was gaining moment by moment. His prayers were to be positive.

Secondly, he was to fill his mind with Scripture. He was to read passages that dealt specifically with his problem (1 Thes. 4:1-7, Gal. 5:16-18, Col. 3:5). He was also to meditate on passages that assured him of God's presence and power in his life (Ps. 57:1-2). Then I challenged him to fast one day each week for the three weeks following. After that, I told him we would talk again.

One month later he returned. Fasting had really been a struggle for him, especially the first day. "I was tempted to give up every hour," he said, "but by the evening of the second day, I knew victory was possible." During this time he said he experienced total freedom from lust, though the temptations never ceased.

This young man walked out of my office free. He decided to continue fasting one day a week, however, as a reminder of what God had done for him. Now his prayers would naturally be full of praise and thanksgiving, for God had delivered him from bondage.

Could one or two drives in your life be out of balance? Sometimes you may win the fight, while other times you lose. This situation does not have to exist. You can have complete victory if you will allow God to help you put all your drives under the Holy Spirit's control. When this happens, you'll find freedom that you never thought was possible.

Control of the Holy Spirit

A third principle is that fasting helps bring our minds, wills, and emotions under the Holy Spirit's control. Fasting allows us to think clearer and quicker. As a result, there is a new and constant awareness of God's presence during times of fasting. His presence becomes more evident even in the midst of our daily routine. During times of fasting, our minds are quicker to discern the things of the Spirit. This is especially important when we're seeking guidance for a big decision.

Aids in Worship

A fourth principle is that fasting is a tremendous aid when we seek the Lord in worship. What would happen if you and I began to fast on Saturdays before we went to the Lord's house on Sunday? What would happen if an entire congregation did this? The worship service would become a *real* worship service. When people begin to fast and pray and seek God, and He becomes the priority of their thinking, feeling, and action, something begins to happen to them and everybody around.

When Jesus spoke about fasting, He didn't say *if* you fast—but *when* you fast. What reasons do we find in Scripture for fasting?

Disciplines the Spirit

Fasting disciplines our spirits toward the things of the Father. When the time came for Jesus to seek direction concerning His ministry, He spent time fasting and praying. For 40 days and nights He disciplined His spirit and body in order to find His Father's will. Though Christ was closer to God than anyone on earth, He still found it necessary to go this extra mile.

He knew that fasting brings one's relationship with God to a point that it becomes an absolute priority. Fasting allows us to discipline ourselves, and therefore places us in a position whereby we can reach our maximum potential both mentally and spiritually.

Many Christians don't see the necessity of fasting. But if Christ found it necessary, then it will be necessary for us too. If we are to reach our maximum potential, we must know what God has to say to us individually. This calls for intense prayer. Fasting intensifies prayer, allowing us to reach into the innermost part of our spirit till we can understand spiritual things that we otherwise could not grasp.

How many times have we said or heard others say, "I just don't know what I'm feeling. I can't seem to figure it out"? Fasting prunes and peels off layer after layer of feelings, attitudes, and experiences till we get to the hard core of what God is trying to say to us. Fasting is the discipline of the spirit.

Finding God's Will

Fasting helps us find God's will. For example, let's say you are contemplating marriage. You don't really know for sure that this is God's will, but you think it might be. You've prayed, and read, and talked to counselors, but you still aren't sure.

Here is a suggestion. Spend three days alone on your face before God, fasting and praying for guidance. Tell Him that you want Him to show you through His Word what you should do. God honors this kind of praying. As you fast and pray He will clear your eyes, your ears, your heart, and your spirit. Your attention will be turned toward Him and you will hear from God as never before. His leading will become clear, and you will be able to follow His plans with complete assurance of His blessings.

Daniel understood this principle. He struggled over a prophecy of Jeremiah. He knew there was something God wanted him to know, but it just would not come clear. So he fasted and prayed before the Lord. He gave up the fulfilling of certain physical appetites in order to find out what God was saying.

We need to ask ourselves: *Do I want to reach my potential for God, or am I willing to be satisfied with just getting by spiritually? Do I desire the applause and praise of others more than the praise of God? Do I want to fulfill my appetites, or do I want to fulfill God's will?*

If we look at our daily schedules, we'll see that we are consumed with fulfilling our fleshly appetites rather than our

spiritual ones. Then we turn right around and complain that
God doesn't speak to us. He seems so far away. If we expect
God to reveal His direction and will for our lives, we must put
Him first. Often this means putting aside the fulfillment of
our physical appetites so that we can focus our attention on
Him.

Aids in Repentance

There is another purpose for fasting. Fasting is often
associated with personal repentance and confession. For
example, let's say you have a habit that you cannot overcome.
You know there is a truth that will set you free, but somehow
you just cannot find it. You've tried everything, yet you still
have no victory.

So you begin to fast. At first it is a struggle as Satan attacks
with everything he knows is effective against you. He says,
"Do you really think this is going to work? What is your
family going to think? And besides, you aren't supposed to
tell anyone, but they already know. You're just wasting your
time."

On and on he goes, up till the moment God reveals to you
how to be free. All fasting will not be this tough. But
remember, the closer you get to victory, the harder Satan will
work to discourage you.

If you have ever tried to fast and pray, and failed to be true
to your commitment, then you've experienced such attacks.
But often we don't recognize our enemy. We become full of
self-condemnation, when actually we should be encouraged
that Satan is worried enough to even bother us. Satan knows
when one of God's children repents with fasting and prayer
that God will cleanse that child and remove the strongholds.
He knows that when we go to God in this way, we'll see
ourselves in a new light. We'll see sin, wickedness, and
carnality in our hearts we have never seen before. So Satan
does anything he can to keep us from getting too serious
about our repenting and confessing.

There is no incident in the Bible of people fasting, praying, and repenting when God did not release His supernatural power in their lives. The same holds true today. If the body of Christ fasted and prayed one day a week, God's power would be released as we have never seen before. Churches would be filled. People would be in no hurry to leave the services. Through our confession and repentance, we would free God to send the revival this world needs so desperately.

Fasting is not necessary every time we confess sin, but it serves as an outward sign of genuine sorrow and grief over sin. It shows God that we are more concerned about correcting our relationship with Him than we are fulfilling our fleshly appetites.

Are you at the point in your life that you say, "I want to be everything God wants me to be, but I just cannot seem to get things straight"? Do you feel as if there is something holding you back? Then I challenge you to spend a day alone with God fasting and praying. Tell your family what your plans are without making a big deal out of it.

If you are having some sort of family problem, it may be a good idea to fast and pray with your spouse. You may even want to include your whole family. Either way, God will do something supernatural in your life and in your family's life.

Protection of a Nation

Frequently the Bible mentions fasting for the protection of a nation. In 2 Chronicles 20, Jehoshaphat called the nation of Israel to a fast after he heard that an enemy was approaching. In desperation he fell on his face and cried out to God before the people. When he finished, God spoke through a prophet who was standing in the congregation.

God told Jehoshaphat to get his army together and march into battle—with the choir and orchestra leading the way. Well, you can imagine how amazed the enemy was when the choir came out first, so amazed that they became confused. God defeated them, but He did not do it the natural and normal way. If God saves this country, He will do it His way.

We would like to see God save our nation by sending a

great spiritual awakening, but we don't know what God's plans are. However, we do know that God honors fasting and praying on behalf of nations. If we get concerned and burdened enough, nobody will have to beg us to fast. It will not even be an effort.

My concern is this: how far must we go as a nation before Christians finally wake up and see what is happening? How far must we go before we fast and pray regularly for God's deliverance? I believe He is waiting on us. But like Jehoshaphat, we must recognize our danger and our weaknesses, and then recognize our Deliverer.

Accomplishing God's Work

Fasting is also mentioned in Scripture in relation to people's concern for accomplishing God's work. Look at Nehemiah's example. When he was serving as the king's cupbearer, he heard news that Jerusalem's walls were broken down and that the gates were burned. He wrote, "And it came to pass, when I heard these words, that I sat down and wept, and mourned certain days, and fasted, and prayed before the God of heaven" (Neh. 1:4). Verses 5 through 11 are a record of his prayer. He fasted and prayed while keeping his burden to himself.

One day the king asked Nehemiah, "Why is your countenance sad?" (2:2) Then Nehemiah became afraid, for it was improper to show grief in the king's presence. People were supposed to be cheerful to keep the king in a good mood.

But Nehemiah's grief was too much to keep inside, so he told the king about his people and their desperate condition. He described the condition of the city and the walls. Then the heathen king asked how he could help Nehemiah. Though taken by surprise at his offer, Nehemiah told how he wanted to return to Jerusalem to rebuild the walls.

The king was faithful to his word, and he let Nehemiah return to Jerusalem. But along with him he sent all the supplies needed to repair the walls and the gates. Then to top it all off, he sent an escort from his own army to guard Nehemiah.

This is a perfect illustration of what happens when God's people fast and pray over a concern for God's work. Today, however, we often try to do God's work in our own strength. We use the world's resources to finance God's work and the world's principles to maintain His work. But God cautions us not to be conformed to the world's ways of doing things. Rather we are to use His principles.

What if Nehemiah had tried to work out a way to rebuild the walls without waiting on God? Where could a slave have gotten that much money? And how could he have left the city without being caught? And even if he had gotten that far, he would have risked being recaptured and put in prison. In other words, God's work would have never been done—not through Nehemiah anyway.

I wonder how much of God's work never gets done, or is delayed, as a result of our wrong thinking. As we do God's work in God's way, we do it in God's power. In His power the impossible becomes reality. We are merely instruments to be used for God's glory.

God wants us to be occupied with the salvation of souls, for it is every Christian's responsibility. The church of the Lord Jesus Christ is larger and richer than it has ever been before. Yet we are falling further and further behind in our calling to fulfill the Great Commission. Why? Because somewhere along the way we lost our dependence on the Holy Spirit, and we have tried to win the world through clever mottos, persuasive speeches, manipulated emotions, and useless gimmicks. But it isn't working.

Spiritual Awakening

I believe God wants to send a spiritual awakening to this nation, but He will not send it till He knows we are ready. We must quit trusting in our strength and our resources, and start pleading with God through fasting and prayer to send us His anointing. Only then will we be prepared to do His work. And only then will God send revival to our land.

But we aren't desperate enough yet. We still have the idea that we can have a revival without making too much of a personal sacrifice. As individuals and as a nation we need to confess and repent of this attitude of pride. Such self-sufficiency keeps God from accomplishing His work through us.

Right before the election of 1980, our church members set aside a period of 10 days to fast and pray. The idea was to have somebody fasting and praying 24 hours a day during the entire 10-day period. One couple misunderstood the announcement and thought they were supposed to fast all 10 days—so they did! When they found out their mistake, they came to tell me what had happened. They were beaming. Both said it was the greatest experience of their lives. They said God used that time to point out some hidden sins in their personal lives that had been affecting their marriage. He cleansed their lives and restored their relationship with each other. They were excited about doing it again.

God wants to do a supernatural work in your life and in the life of your family. He wants you to have His best. It is my prayer that you will allow God to exercise His power through your life in the way He sees fit. Most likely, it will mean making some kind of sacrifice—perhaps through prayer and fasting. But is there any price too great when we consider what Christ did for us?

4
A Prayer Burden

The words of Nehemiah the son of Hachaliah. And it came to pass in the month Chisleu, in the twentieth year, as I was in Shushan the palace, that Hanani, one of my brethren came, he and certain men of Judah; and I asked them concerning the Jews that had escaped, which were left of the captivity, and concerning Jerusalem. And they said unto me, "The remnant that are left of the captivity there in the province are in great affliction and reproach: the wall of Jerusalem also is broken down, and the gates thereof are burned with fire." And it came to pass, when I heard these words, that I sat down and wept, and mourned certain days, and fasted, and prayed before the God of heaven, and said, "I beseech thee, O Lord God of heaven, the great and terrible God, that keepeth covenant and mercy for them that love Him and observe His commandments: let Thine ear now be attentive, and Thine eyes open, that Thou mayest hear the prayer of Thy servant, which I pray before Thee now, day and night, for the children of Israel Thy servants, and confess the sins of the children of Israel, which we have sinned

41

against Thee: both I and my father's house have sinned. We have dealt very corruptly against Thee, and have not kept the commandments, nor the statutes , nor the judgments, which Thou commandedst Thy servant Moses. Remember, I beseech Thee, the word that Thou commandedst Thy servant Moses, saying, 'If ye transgress, I will scatter you abroad among the nations: but if ye turn unto Me, and keep My commandments, and do them; though there were of you cast out unto the uttermost part of the heaven, yet will I gather them from thence, and will bring them unto the place that I have chosen to set My name there.' Now these are Thy servants and Thy people, whom Thou hast redeemed by Thy great power, and by Thy strong hand. O Lord, I beseech Thee, let now Thine ear be attentive to the prayer of Thy servant, and to the prayer of Thy servants, who desire to fear Thy name: and prosper, I pray Thee, Thy servant this day, and grant him mercy in the sight of this man." For I was the king's cupbearer.

Nehemiah 1:1-11

This story was told to me by a friend, who at the time of the incident was pastoring a church in Miami:

One Monday afternoon, around 4:00, a woman in his congregation was preparing dinner when she suddenly became concerned about my friend Jack. She tried to put him out of her mind, but for some reason she couldn't stop thinking about him.

So she left the kitchen, went into her bedroom, and began praying. As she prayed she began crying. She pleaded with God to sustain him in this crisis, whatever it was. This went on for 30 minutes. Then, as suddenly as it came, the burden left her. She went back to her cooking and didn't think about it again till the next Sunday when she saw Jack in church.

She told Jack what had happened and asked him if anything

was wrong. With a look of amazement, he shared his harrowing experience.

On that same Monday, he was flying his private single-engine plane from Miami to Ft. Pierce, Florida. Being in a hurry, he failed to check his fuel.

About halfway to Ft. Pierce, his engine began to sputter and finally quit. He looked at his watch—it was 4 P.M. As his plane was losing altitude, Jack started praying and looking for a place to land. But there was no suitable place in sight.

As Jack prepared for a crash landing, he spotted a field that had just been plowed and cleared for planting. By that time his aircraft was losing altitude rapidly and the field was still a long way off. Jack knew the outcome of this situation was totally in the Lord's hands.

Jack made it to the field. When his plane finally came to a halt, the nose cone was resting gently against a tree. Neither Jack nor his plane were in any way damaged. As Jack thanked God for saving him, he looked at his watch—it was 4:30.

As Jack concluded his account of the previous Monday, both he and the woman had tears in their eyes. She had been an instrument of God in a crisis. He had been the focus of God's love and watchcare. Together they were an example of how God uses prayer burdens to care for those He loves.

Praying with a burden is probably the most neglected aspect of prayer. As a result, we often pray burdenless prayers. We repeat the same old requests over and over, but with no heart or sense of urgency.

To illustrate the principle of praying with a burden, we return to the story of Nehemiah. Nehemiah was a slave in Babylon, serving as cupbearer to the king. Everything was going along fine till some of his friends from Jerusalem went to Babylon and told him about the awful condition of the city. He became burdened and wept and mourned.

The Source of a Burden
According to Scripture, burdens come from one of three sources. Sometimes we feel burdened as a result of

unconfessed sin. The way to handle this is simply to confess the sin and move on. Sometimes we feel burdened because of *negative attitudes.* These attitudes can either be ours, or attitudes someone else has toward us. Either way, wrong thinking can become an unnecessary burden, one that will eventually lead to ruin.

At other times *God* gives us a burden. A burden from God is a heaviness of heart and spirit; it is an expression of God's concern regarding sin in a person's life or a particular need he may have. Its main function is to get us on our knees before the Lord, praying in accordance with His will.

There are several aspects of a prayer burden that we must understand if we are to recognize a burden from God and respond to it properly. Once we get these key principles implanted in our minds, we will see lasting fruit as a result of our God-given burdens.

A burden from God is always directed toward a specific need—toward something or someone He wants to change. The burden may be in response to sin in the life of the one with the burden, or it may be in response to sin in the life of a friend. In Nehemiah's case, the burden was a result of God's sorrow over the sad state of affairs in Jerusalem. God wanted those circumstances changed, so He burdened Nehemiah.

Evidence of God's Intentions

When God burdens our hearts to pray, He intends to do something about the thing He has burdened us for. If God burdens your heart about someone who is lost, this is evidence that God plans to save that person. Often God will use the person He burdens to help accomplish His will. If God burdens you to pray for someone who has a financial need, God probably wants you to help meet that need in a material way as well as through prayer.

Prayer always begins with God. For instance, let's say God sees you have a need. God begins searching for someone who is available to receive the burden. He may choose someone who is a close friend, or someone you hardly know. Either way, He looks for someone who is living an obedient, godly life—someone He can trust to follow through once he receives the burden.

Once He finds someone and gives them the burden, that person begins to have a heavy heart for you. God increases the burden and its intensity till it becomes very real and that person understands the importance of his sensitivity to God's will. He begins to intercede on your behalf as the Lord leads. This frees God to work on behalf of his prayers and He meets your need. It may be met through the person praying, or through some other means.

How It Works

In essence, this process works like a triangle: God burdens person A; person A prays for person B; person B has his need met by God; and person A is blessed by seeing an answer to prayer. Often when God meets our needs we get the impression that it was a result of our prayers only. But we never know who God has burdened for us. When we get to heaven and see who was praying for us, and when they prayed, we will be both surprised and humbled. None of us are sufficient in ourselves—we need each others' prayers.

But why should an omnipotent God use this triangle of prayer to accomplish His will? He can answer prayers without outside help, can't He? If God sees my need, why should He bother anyone else with it?

Sure, God could do it all without us. But He has chosen this method to allow us to be blessed by seeing Him work in others' lives. He wants us involved with each other on a spiritual basis—loving and encouraging each other. God uses this triangle of prayer to unify us. He allows us to be a part of somebody else's blessing by involving us in the answer to the prayer. This is the very nature of a prayer burden.

How a Burden Is Communicated

We know that all true prayer burdens are from God, but how does God communicate His burdens to us? Many times He will use something someone says. On other occasions God may speak to us directly through His Word or in some other way when we are still and listening.

At 8:00 one morning a man called me and said, "Charles, I have hesitated to call you because I didn't know how you would respond to what I am about to say. God told me to call and tell you to cancel everything you have planned for the day and spend your time praying."

My first reaction to my friend's call was to go on with business as usual and plan another day for prayer. But God confirmed His instructions in my heart so strongly that I could not resist with a clear conscience.

I called my secretary and told her to cancel everything on my schedule for that day. Then I went to my study and spent the day on my knees. As soon as I started reading the Scriptures, it was as if every verse said, "Dear Charles." I knew God had something special for me.

It took several weeks for God to show me what He was saying. But I believe that day of fasting and prayer was the spark. And it all started because God's burden over my need was communicated to me through a friend's inspired advice.

I believe God could have told me directly, without the intervention of another person, but in this case He chose to use a friend. The Lord must have known that either I was not listening, or my arrangements were so fixed that it would take something unusual to get my attention. But God also knew that this episode would strengthen and deepen my relationship with my friend.

Regardless of how we receive a prayer burden, it is ultimately from God. It may come as a sudden heaviness of heart, or it may come slowly, growing in intensity. Some burdens come both ways. Be careful not to mistake a burden for some physical or emotional problem. Sometimes a burden will get a person down to where he thinks it is a case of depression. But instead of getting down in the dumps, we are to get down on our knees.

The Weight of a Burden

The next aspect of a prayer burden we must understand is the weight of a burden. In Nehemiah's case, the burden was so great that it caused him to weep and mourn. In fact, he could barely go about his responsibilities. And when he did, his face was so sad that the king noticed.

Not all burdens will take so great a toll on us, but some *will* cause us to stop everything. When the burden is so heavy, Satan is usually quick to tell us to shake it off and keep moving. "You're too busy to worry about that now," he says. But in spite of our pressing responsibilities, we must take the time to get away and spend a few hours or days alone with God in prayer.

All burdens will not require days or even hours of prayer; some burdens may be for something God wants you to do in that moment. For instance, He may burden you to call a friend or give something to the poor. These types of burdens may be understood immediately without a long process of seeking God. But we need to be willing to spend longer times with God when necessary.

Timing Is Important

Once you have decided to take time to seek the Lord, Satan will tempt you to put it off. But timing is important when following up a burden. A few summers ago, my son and some friends went rafting down a white-water river in North Carolina. While on the river, they were involved in rescuing another party of rafters who had lost control of their raft and were being swept toward the most dangerous part of the river. During the rescue, one boy who tried to swim across the river injured his knee and was taken to the hospital.

That evening when the group returned home, a mother of one of the girls asked if everyone was alright. Her voice showed such concern that it was obvious she had been worried. After being questioned about her surprising concern, she explained that during the day the Lord had placed a burden on her heart to pray for the group's safety. As she prayed, the Lord revealed to her that there had been an accident of some kind and that someone had injured a leg.

This wise mother knew the importance of timing in following up a burden. She allowed God to intercede through her during the time of crisis. God used her prayers to keep a bad situation from getting worse.

Worry vs Burden

At this point, we should distinguish between a worry and a prayer burden. A worry is self-centered, while a burden is God-centered. Worrying focuses our attention on *our* circumstances; God wants our attention focused on *Him*. In fact, He doesn't ever want us to focus on the person or thing He burdens us about.

The intensity of a burden will be determined by two factors: the magnitude of the situation God wants to deal with and the immediacy with which God wants to deal with it. When my friend called he said, "This morning you are to start praying." Immediately I was overwhelmed with a tremendous sense of God's presence and an awesomeness at the burden God was placing on me. God wanted me to do something right then. In Nehemiah's case, the magnitude of the job to be done made his burden heavy. He had a whole city to rebuild with no idea of how to get it done.

Sometimes the immediacy of a thing is important because God sees we are about to run off a cliff. We are headed in a particular direction in life and everything is going great. Then all of a sudden we sense something isn't right. God burdens our hearts. We feel Him plowing us up and causing us to feel unsure about things.

We examine our lives for sin. Everything checks out, but still something is wrong. This is when we need to stop and ask, "Lord, what are You trying to say?" Only when we stop everything and get quiet do we give God a chance to tell us what He is burdening us about.

God will show us if we are running in the wrong direction. He will reveal to us the direction He would have us go. So besides getting us involved in each other's lives, a prayer burden may be put on our hearts to keep us from making a wrong decision.

The Length of a Burden

Some burdens last longer than others. The length depends on the magnitude of the burden and our response to what God is saying. Sometimes we resist a burden, which causes God's prolonging to get us in a position where we will listen. We should keep in mind that whenever God burdens our hearts about a particular situation, the burden is evidence that He is already working.

This fact should encourage us to pray with perfect faith. A burden is a promise of God's hand in a particular matter. God does His work primarily through the prayers of His children. By giving us a burden, He gives us an opportunity to build our faith. How? By allowing us to pray for something He has already started to answer. When God lays a burden on our hearts and we follow it up faithfully, it is as good as done. There is no need to pray, "If it be Thy will." We *know* it is His will, simply because He has placed the burden on our hearts.

There have been times when God has placed a burden on my heart that lasted for months. At other times burdens have lasted only a few hours. If God requires a drastic change in my life, the burden will stay with me till the change is made. He will keep the pressure on till I focus on Him and seek His guidance.

Nehemiah's burden lasted a long time—so long that it had affected his physical appearance. But while Nehemiah had been praying and seeking God's guidance, God was already working with the king. We don't know in what way, but *something* had been going on. The king not only let Nehemiah and his people go home, but he gave them all the building materials they needed. Then to top if all off, he sent an armed escort. The king would never have made such a big sacrifice on the spur of the moment just because one of his servants looked a little depressed. God had prepared his heart.

It was only after Nehemiah saw God accomplish all of this that the burden lifted. Nehemiah had been faithful to the burden God had laid on his heart. He was not only faithful in his prayers, but when he saw an opportunity to be used, he took it. He made himself available to be part of the answer to his own prayer.

Sharing Our Burdens

Sharing burdens is a tool God uses to get His work done. But we must be extremely sensitive to God's guidance when we share burdens. Some burdens need to be shared, while others need to be kept private. When we share a burden it must be done in the spirit of genuine encouragement and love. There must be no criticism.

Many times God will want us to share the burden with only the person we have been burdened for. The timing is very important, because while He is working on us, He is working on them. When God gets both parties ready, then He will allows us to share our burden. Often, when we share a burden, it will be an encouragement to the one we are burdened for. People who are in need or hurting need to know they are being prayed for.

Some burdens need to be shared with many people. For instance, if you found out that one of your friends was sick, you would feel burdened to pray. In fact, your concern would not only express itself through your prayers, but also through your sharing that need with others who could pray. By sharing these types of burdens, God uses us to burden others to pray. God burdened Nehemiah's friends, who in turn shared their burden with Nehemiah. God used this sharing of a burden to lay the same burden on Nehemiah. As a result, the walls of Jerusalem were rebuilt.

I have a personal burden for this nation. I believe this is a burden every American should help shoulder. It grieves my spirit when I see Americans, especially Christians, who don't feel any burden for America. This is the type of burden that should be shared with everyone.

Personal Blessing

When we follow up a prayer burden and focus on God, we see Him from a new perspective. When this happens we see ourselves from a new perspective. As a result, all that is hidden in our hearts is revealed. As we pray for someone else, God cleanses us so we can hear what He is saying. When a burden, comes, a time of cleansing always follows. Perhaps this is one reason we run from burdens—we don't like to be cleansed. But God knows the cleaner and more Spirit-filled we are, the more effectively we can pray.

As a result of God cleansing us, we feel a new sense of closeness to Him. We find ourselves loving Him more and serving Him more faithfully. Not only do we love *Him* more, but also those around us. With this renewed love for others, we eagerly follow up the burdens God lays on our hearts. A burden, then, is given for the spiritual benefit of everyone involved. When we refuse to take up a burden, we in turn miss a blessing.

Right now your heart may be heavy with a burden from the Lord. You've been trying to shake it off. Maybe you even thought you were ill. The answer is to get on your face before God and tell Him you're willing to receive any burden He has for you. Tell Him you'll stick with it till He accomplishes His purpose.

When you do this, you place yourself in a position to be used by God in someone else's life—either directly or indirectly. But you also allow God to begin cleansing you more deeply than you've ever been cleansed before. You open yourself up to great spiritual blessings.

Are you willing to pray this prayer? *Lord, I am available for any burden You wish to share with me. Don't spare the weight. Use me to the maximum.*

If this is really your heart's desire, when you get to heaven you will be amazed at what God did with you as a result of your availability to shoulder His burdens.

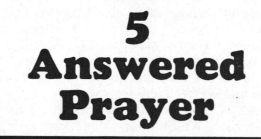

5
Answered
Prayer

Ask, and it shall be given you; seek, and ye shall
find; knock, and it shall be opened unto you: for
every one that asketh receiveth; and he that seeketh
findeth; and to him that knocketh it shall be opened.
Or what man is there of you, whom if his son ask
bread, will he give him a stone? Or if he ask a fish,
will he give him a serpent? If ye then, being evil,
know how to give good gifts unto your children, how
much more shall your Father which is in heaven give
good things to them that ask Him?

Matthew 7:7-11

This passage makes prayer appear to be simply a cause and
effect process. Ask and then receive—as if there is nothing
else to it. But often this doesn't happen when we pray. We
ask, but we see no results.

We are all interested in answered prayer, but our
unanswered prayers have led many of us not to expect God to
answer every time we pray. In fact, when a prayer *is*
answered, we are surprised. We know the Bible teaches that
God answers prayer. We know He has answered some
prayers in our lives. We have seen Him answer the prayers of

others. But we still struggle and wonder why He does not answer all the time.

An Encouragement to Pray

First Jesus encourages us to pray. He tells us to ask, seek, and knock. We ask for things, we seek understanding, and we knock on doors of opportunity that lay before us. The Lord is saying that in every area of life we can find what we are looking for by talking to the heavenly Father.

Some people question whether we should ask God for material things. The answer is found in verses 9 and 10. Wise parents do everything in their power to satisfy their children's needs. This goes for material needs as well as nutritional and spiritual needs. According to verse 11, the material gifts we give our children are proof that God wants to give to us in the same way, but to a greater degree. Do we have a privilege that God has deprived Himself of? No! In fact, there is no way we can outgive God, materially or any other way.

Are We Worth It?

Another hang-up some people have is in regard to their unworthiness to have God answer their prayers. But the basis of all God's answered prayer is His love for us. Calvary settled the question of worth once and for all. According to His love, we are worthy of the greatest gift He had to give—His Son. After that, anything else we ask for is secondary.

Why do we have so much trouble believing God for the minor things in life? It is Satan who says, "Who do you think you are, to ask God for anything?"

To this question there is only one answer: "I am a child of the King. I am so worthy in the eyes of God, He sent His only begotten Son to die for me. If He died for me, certainly He will give me whatever else I need."

There are two opposite schools of thought concerning God's attitude toward blessing us on earth. One group believes we should live in poverty, suffer persecution, and die in poverty as a sacrifice to God. The opposite group believes that all we have to do is ask God and He starts pouring on the blessings; He will give us whatever we ask. According to this group, all we must do is think right. But both of these views are extremes. Neither has the proper balance.

God's Attitude toward Blessing His Children

God loves us and wants to meet all our needs. He wants to give us the desires of our hearts (Ps. 37:4). But God also desires that we seek His face, not just His hand. When our prayers are filled with *I want*, chances are our eyes are on the blessing, and not on God. Just as God gives out of love, He desires that we love Him in return. When we love Him, we will seek Him and not just His blessings. To redirect our attention, He will often close the windows of heaven. Otherwise, we would continue on blindly in our error and never seek to know Him the way He intends.

Our heavenly Father loves us so much He wants us to have what we seek. But He will always measure our desires against what He knows is best for us. That's why it is foolish for us to complain when God doesn't answer certain prayers. Since His decisions are for our best interest, then we should never try to talk Him into giving us what He has already said we cannot have.

When my family and I first moved to Atlanta, we looked for over a month before we found a suitable house. We had been living with friends up till then. When my wife told me she had found just what we were looking for, I was thrilled.

We prayed and felt like this was of the Lord, so we applied for a loan. We asked God every day to get that loan approved for us. We really believed He would; we even thanked Him in advance.

One week later, the bank told me our loan had been turned down. This came as a real shock. To this day, I still don't know the reason they turned us down. And we couldn't understand what God was up to. "Why didn't He answer our prayer?" we asked.

God answered that question the next day by sending a

tremendous rainstorm. The basement of the house we almost bought was flooded with a foot of water. We had planned to use the basement for a study and for storage. But God was watching out for us even when we misunderstood His will. One week later we found the right house, and enjoyed living there for eight years.

Now that we understand the foundation of God's love for us, we need to understand how to get into a position to allow Him to answer our prayers. The problem is not in God's ability. He can do more than we can ask or think. In fact the problem is not with God at all; the problem is with us.

There are six conditions that must be true in our lives if God is going to answer our prayers.

Right Relationship
First of all, we must have a right relationship with Him. The psalmist wrote, "If I regard iniquity in my heart, the Lord will not hear me" (Ps. 66:18). This does not mean every time we make a mistake God says, "Close up the windows and shut all the doors, no more blessings for that person." If this were true, none of us would ever get anywhere in life.

But if we aim at evil and willfully choose to do evil, the windows of heaven will be shut and God's fellowship broken. This doesn't mean that every time we stumble spiritually God refuses to hear our prayers. He understands where we are and the difficulties we face. But He allows no compromise concerning known sin in our lives.

We must set our sights on God. He must be our aim in life. We must seek to live our lives according to the precepts of His Word, and according to the guidance He gives us.

Right Method
The right method answers the question of how we go to the Lord in prayer. The key is to be specific. Jesus says that whatever we believe Him for will become ours in reality. "Therefore I say unto you, all things for which you pray and ask, believe that you have received them, and they shall be

granted you" (Mark 11:24, NASB). In other words, whatever we are able to visualize by faith as ours, God will make it so.

We are not to windowshop when we pray. "Lord, help all the missionaries, and Mom and Dad. Bless the church . . . ." Praying like that is like walking into a restaurant and telling the waitress we want "food and drink." When we pray vague prayers it shows that the requests don't really mean much to us. Yet we expect God to get all excited and do something.

Sure, God knows what we are thinking. The problem is that most of the time we don't have anything specific in mind. God could answer prayers like that and we would never know about it. Not only that, He would get no glory, and we would receive no blessing from seeing a prayer answered.

When the time came for me to buy my daughter a car, I asked her what she wanted. She had been praying and she knew the exact year, model, color, and interior of car she wanted. So we began looking. I had taught her to be specific in her prayers but I had no idea she would be so specific. Regardless of what kind of car we saw or how good the price was, she stuck by what she originally asked God for. This went on for months.

Then one night my son was looking through the want ads and he found a car just like Becky was looking for. It was the right make, color, model, and year. We went to look at it that night, and after talking with the owner for just a few minutes, we knew it was the right car. It didn't take much prayer to know if we were making the right decision; all the praying had been done.

God encourages us to pray specific prayers. Once we decide on something, we must stick with it in our prayers; otherwise we demonstrate a lack of faith. The psalmist does not say, "He shall give thee the *needs* of thine heart." But rather he writes, "He shall give thee the *desires* of thine heart" (Ps. 37:4). We must understand that what we are asking for is not really the issue. It is the attitude of our heart that matters. God wants to bless His children, but the relationship and method must be right.

The Right Request

The third aspect of prayer we must understand is how to make the right request. "And this is the confidence that we have in Him, that, if we ask any thing according to His will, He heareth us" (1 John 5:14). We must ask according to His will. But how do we know if our request is in His will?

First we must express our desire for what we want from Him. Sometimes we feel guilty for wanting certain things, so we disguise our desires. But if we are to know God's attitude about the thing, we must admit our desires. Then we must be willing for Him to bring us into complete neutrality—to the point where it really doesn't matter one way or the other. Neutrality means that we want what God wants more than what we want. This may take some time and prayer, but it is an essential step in finding God's will.

Sometimes as soon as we get neutral about something, we lose all our desire for it. This is one way God shows us His will. At other times once we are neutral, God restrains our spirit about the request; we just won't feel peace in asking for it any longer. Neutrality removes some of the emotion attached to the request. When our emotions are reset on the Lord by becoming neutral, the fog of uncertainty begins to clear. As a result, we can see God's direction more clearly.

The Right Formula

When most of us pray, we add "in Jesus' name" to the end of our prayers. For some it is a habit, for others it is considered a magic phrase that assures an answer. We read John 14:14 and mistakenly decide that the only qualification to having our prayers answered is to say, "in Jesus' name." This is a mistake. For there is another qualification: we must abide (John 15:7).

Praying in Jesus' name is more than a phrase we add to a prayer; it is the character of the prayer itself. To pray in Jesus' name means that we are asking something because it is in character with what Jesus would ask if He were in our circumstances. It means that the prayer is in keeping with His nature and character as He lives His life through us. Since He indwells us, He not only desires to live through us, but to intercede through us as well.

Many times we make what may appear to be mundane requests. But they are real needs to us, and God is willing to meet them. Whether they are for spiritual or material needs, it makes little difference to Him; He is our loving Father who delights in meeting all our needs. But before we add "in Jesus' name," on the end, we must make sure everything in the prayer is in keeping with His character.

Right Attitudes

In the Book of James the attitude we are to have when making requests is described. When we come to God and doubt if we are in His will in making a request, we are wavering Christians. Often we feel confident about making a request, and then we talk to friends and they tell us we are wrong. Back and forth we are tossed; should we, or shouldn't we? James wrote about the wavering Christian, "Let not that man think that he shall receive anything of the Lord" (James 1:7).

Doubt and prayer do not mix. Doubt comes from relying on feelings and others' opinions. A man whose faith wavers in prayer is a "double-minded man" and is "unstable in all his ways" (v. 8). He is not just unstable in his prayer life, but in *all* his ways. Our faith in God determines our course in life. For if our faith in Him wavers, where else will we put our security?

In the winter of 1981 our church was offered the opportunity to purchase a block and a half of property adjacent to our present facilities. The cost was $2,850,000 in cash at closing. The bank was willing to lend us the money at 21 percent interest. But I didn't believe that God wanted us to borrow the money. He wanted to build our faith.

In the previous 12 months, our congregation had given over $1,200,000 for additional property and renovation. Two weeks before the deadline we had only $125,000 more. It looked impossible, especially in light of how much the people had already given.

On Sunday morning I preached from 2 Chronicles 29, which is the account of Israel's response to David's challenge to provide funds to build the temple. At the close of the first morning service, a young man offered his wedding band for the fund. It was the only possession of any value he and his wife had. They had been robbed the week before and lost everything else.

At the second service, I preached the same sermon and shared the sacrificial spirit of the couple. At the close of the message, I invited people to be saved or to unite with our fellowship. People lined up across the front of the sanctuary and up and down the aisles. They gave diamond rings, bracelets, pendants, watches, necklaces; they promised cars, campers, stocks and bonds, etc. By the following Friday we had $1,350,000.

When I thought about how much money was given and how much more we needed my faith would nose-dive. But when I spent time alone with God in prayer, it was always the same message: "Trust Me."

I soon saw a pattern. When I would try to figure out just how we could come up with the money, my faith would waver. But as long as I accepted my utter helplessness, my faith soared like an eagle.

When I stepped into the pulpit on the following Sunday with the deadline 24 hours away, we still needed an additional $1,500,000. As I looked out across the sea of faces, it all seemed so impossible. But I knew what I had to do. God and I had settled that the day before.

I had spent that Saturday in prayer wrestling with my weak and wavering faith. God spoke to me very clearly. I must publicly declare that we would not borrow any money; we must trust the Lord to provide our needs and to prove Himself faithful. He pointed me to Isaiah 50:7-11 for a word of encouragement and warning.

As I shared this challenge with the people, I made it clear that we wouldn't borrow any money. "We must burn every bridge and cut off every avenue of escape. Our faith must be in Him and Him alone," I said.

I held up a strand of hair and cut it with scissors as a symbol of cutting off all routes of retreat. When I did that, something happened to the congregation. They were released. By that Sunday evening they gave an additional $1 million. Thirty minutes before the deadline we had our $2,850,000.

What then is the right attitude? Jesus summed it up. "What things soever ye desire, when ye pray, believe that you receive them, and ye shall have them" (Mark 11:24). Faith is the capacity to visualize what is not as if it had already happened. Once we visualize it, we must act on what we know to be true by faith. Our faith must not be based on how we feel or what our five senses tell us, but on what God says in His Word. Feelings and circumstances change, but God never changes. The right attitude is one of faith.

Right Motive

Finally, we must have right motives. Christ said, "Let your light so shine before men, that they may see your good works, and glorify your Father which is in heaven" (Matt. 5:16). Our motives for everything we do must be to glorify the Father.

Can a prayer for some mundane, seemingly unimportant material thing give glory to God? Yes! But only if we are willing to share the need or desire being met as a testimony to others of God's faithfulness. In this way, God will receive glory out of any prayer He answers.

When people hear of a specific request being answered, their faith is strengthened. What we ask for is really insignificant compared with the glory God will receive. When we set our sights in prayer on giving God glory rather than just getting what we're asking for, God will delight in answering our prayers.

If we want our prayers to affect God we must (1) begin with a right relationship with Him through Jesus Christ; (2) make specific requests; (3) pray according to His will for us; (4) pray in Jesus' name and in keeping with His character; (5) ask in faith that is based on God's Word, not on feelings or on others' opinions; (6) pray with the right motives. All we do, say, and pray must be to the glory of God.

If your prayers aren't being answered, check out these six conditions. It is God's desire and joy to answer your prayers. I pray that you will put yourself in a position that will allow Him to do just that.

6
Why Our Prayers Are Unanswered

But without faith it is impossible to please Him: for he that cometh to God must believe that He is, and that He is a rewarder of them that diligently seek Him.

Hebrews 11:6

A member of our church came into my office one afternoon weeping over her husband's decision to divorce her. She could not understand what had prompted his decision, but she was willing to do whatever she could to rebuild their marriage. After we talked, we both decided to commit ourselves to pray.

Frances was fervent in her prayers. She fasted and prayed with such urgency that many of her friends joined her prayer campaign. Soon, everyone involved believed that her husband would change his mind and that God would rebuild Frances' home.

Six months later, however, the divorce was finalized. Frances and her 14-year-old son were left with almost nothing. Still she persevered in prayer, sure that God would soften her husband's heart. Once again, people all over the church joined with Frances in prayer.

Then one morning Frances' husband called and told her about his plans to marry a younger woman. This devastated Frances. When she came into my office later that day, she looked at me through swollen eyes and asked, "Dr. Stanley, why didn't God answer my prayer?"

Frances' question is one that has crossed the mind of every child of God who has prayed seemingly fruitless prayers. Many people ignore unanswered prayer. But in a case such as Frances', the hurt was too big to ignore. Why *didn't* God answer her prayer?

There are things we will never know in this lifetime. But as to the issue of unanswered prayer, God has not left us to wonder. Prayer is not meant to be a game of hit or miss. We aren't slaves left to catch crumbs from the Master's table when He chooses to throw them our way (John 15:15).

Prayer is a child making a request of the Father. And just like any good earthly father, our heavenly Father is willing to tell us why we cannot have certain things we ask for. But before He will tell us, we must ask (James 4:2).

God *does* answer all prayers; He answers *yes, no,* or *wait.* Let's look at those instances when God says *no.* All of us have asked God for things at one time or another and not received what we asked for. We can make as many excuses as we want, but the truth is that God didn't do what we asked Him to do.

Usually when a prayer is answered *no,* we look for sin in our lives. Sometimes this *is* the problem, but many times there is nothing to confess. Yet our prayers still are answered *no.* Let's address this question first: Why does God answer *no,* when to the best of our knowledge we are absolutely clean before Him?

We Must Seek God

God wants us to seek Him more than anything else, even more than we seek answers to prayer. When we come to God in prayer, sometimes our hearts are so full of what we want that we leave God out. Our minds become consumed with the gift rather than the Giver.

This is the basic problem with most prayers. Every other reason we discuss concerning unanswered prayer in some way or another relates back to this. If we are not careful, God becomes a means to an end. But God desires to be the end; it is His desire that we seek Him, and Him alone.

God has predestined us, according to His will, to be conformed to the image of His Son (Rom. 8:29). In God's eyes, the most important thing is that we experience Christ's life in us. This does not necessarily mean He is going to give us everything we ask for. On the contrary, He will only allow us to have those things that are in keeping with His ultimate will.

Unfortunately for us, we forget the big picture in our prayers. We focus on our immediate needs and desires and forget what God is ultimately trying to do—conform us to His image (Col. 3:10). Even when our sins are all confessed, and nothing is standing in the way of our relationship with the Father, He will withhold answers to prayer if He sees we need to refocus our attention on Him.

We Must Trust Him

God also withholds answers to teach us to trust Him. If God gave us everything we wanted every time we asked Him for something, what would happen? Before long, we would take Him for granted. As a result, we would miss out on one of God's greatest blessings—learning to trust Him.

Receiving something the minute we ask for it requires no faith. Yet without faith it is impossible to please Him (Heb. 11:6). God wants to know if we still believe He will keep His word when we have no tangible evidence to hold onto. We are usually tossed to and fro between what God's Word says and what we see and hear. But God uses this struggle to build our faith (James 1:2-3). To quit asking and believing is to call God a liar. To quit praying and believing is to give more credit to our understanding of a situation than to God's omnipotent wisdom.

God does not withhold His answers to taunt us or to toy with our emotions. By withholding His answers, He teaches us to persist in prayer, to keep our eyes focused on Him, and to ignore our feelings. He desires for us to believe Him strictly on the basis of what He says in His Word, regardless of what we see. As we allow God to prove Himself faithful in situation after situation, it becomes easier to trust Him.

He Is Preparing Us

Another reason God withholds answers is because He is in the process of preparing us. Many young people pray and pray that the Lord will send a marriage partner. As they get into their late 20s many question God's interest in their situations. They say, "What is God waiting for?" He may be waiting till He knows they are ready.

As I grow older and look back on life, it is clear that if God had answered certains prayers according to my timing, I would have missed His best in every case. Much of what we pray for is in the will of God, but our timing is off.

Let us say, for instance, your five-year-old son wants a pocketknife and a flashlight. You might not mind giving him the flashlight, but he needs to grow up a little before you can trust him with the knife. In the same way, God is waiting for us to grow spiritually in some areas before He can allow us to experience all the spiritual and material blessings He has in store (Eph. 1:3).

Sometimes God Has Something Better

A fourth reason God withholds answers to our prayers is because He wants to give us something better than we asked for. It may be more than we deserve, more than we ask for, and more than we expect.

One beautiful example of this is the story of Lazarus (John 11). If Jesus had healed Lazarus immediately, we would have missed one of Jesus' greatest miracles. But Jesus seemingly ignored Mary and Martha's pleas to save their brother. Just like us, they didn't understand why Jesus waited. But which is the greater blessing, having a man healed or having him raised from the dead? What at first was interpreted as insensitivity turned out to be a glorious experience for everyone involved.

In 1971 our church's television broadcast was taken off the air because of conflict within the church. After the conflict was resolved, we asked the same network if they would reschedule us at the same broadcast time they had given us before. But they refused to even sell us the time.

We believed God wanted us on television, but for some reason things were not working out. So we prayed that God would once again allow us to begin a television ministry. When we started praying, we thought something would open up soon. But it was a year before anything happened.

One year later we were invited by two different stations to participate in their weekly programming. Instead of being on in black and white like before, our broadcast was in color. One opportunity led to another till today our service is broadcast by satellite all over the nation.

God didn't answer our prayer to be put right back on the air for a reason. He waited and provided us with something much better than we asked for.

These are four reasons God withholds a blessing or answer to prayer when the condition of our heart is not the deciding factor. God's perspective is more all-encompassing than ours; He has His overall purpose for our lives in mind.

It would be great to say that these are the only four reasons God doesn't answer prayer, but there are more. These next seven reasons involve areas we must deal with before God will answer our prayers, and in some cases, before He will even hear our prayers.

Family Relationships

First, prayers are hindered when our home relationships are not right (1 Peter 3:1-7). Think about it: how can we have fellowship with a loving heavenly Father who is forgiving and gracious, and at the same time treat our family members with no consideration? If we allow resentment, bitterness, and indifference to build up between us and members of our families, then our prayers will be hindered. The word *hindered* in verse 7 means to put an obstacle in the way of something. Our conflicts at home may be insurmountable obstacles to our prayers.

I have heard story after story of people who received answers to prayer after they made things right at home. A close friend of mine was constantly struggling to keep his head above water in his business. We had prayed together many times for God to restore his failing business. But regardless of how much or how earnestly we prayed, things didn't change.

Then one day he shared how the Lord had convicted him about some areas in his marriage that he had refused to deal with. These were problems he knew existed but had done nothing about. When he dealt with these problems, God renewed his relationship with his wife. In addition, his business turned completely around. Soon things were better financially than ever before. But more importantly his home, which had been a place of constant conflict, became a place of peace.

Unresolved horizontal conflicts make for unresolved vertical conflicts. As long as things aren't right between us and our families, things won't be right between us and God. If God answers our prayers while we are out of fellowship with other people, He would in a sense be condoning our disobedience. But God will never condone or overlook sin; He hates sin. Our disobedience directly opposes what He ultimately wants to accomplish in our lives. Therefore, it must be dealt with. So what does God do? He closes the door of heaven and locks it up till we get our family relationships straightened out.

Someone may say, "I have had unresolved conflicts with my family for a long time and God has answered *my* prayers." This may appear to be true, but according to Scripture, God will not hear that person's prayers. We forget that other people are praying too, and not only that, but God may be showing mercy to other members of our families while He waits for us to get straightened out. Regardless of what we

think is happening, God won't answer our own prayers if we
have unresolved family conflicts.

I cannot go home on Sunday and yell at my wife for burning
the chicken and then expect God to hear me when I ask Him
to bless the meal. That is hypocrisy. The church is so weak
because there is so much prayerlessness. People are still
talking to God, but God is not listening. When there are
difficulties and heartaches at home, we must confess to each
other right then and there; we must ask for forgiveness when
it is necessary. If we regard iniquity in our hearts—bitterness,
wrong attitudes, or an ungrateful spirit—heaven will be
closed to our prayers.

Jesus said, "For if ye forgive men their trespasses, your
heavenly Father will also forgive you; but if ye forgive not
men their trespasses, neither will your Father forgive your
trespasses" (Matt. 6:14-15). If we have an unforgiving spirit
toward somebody, that in itself is a sin. Therefore, if we
confess our sins and yet refuse to forgive our brother or sister,
then we have not repented of having an unforgiving spirit.
This will be a hindrance to our prayers.

For years people will cling to unconfessed bitterness and
hatred toward a family member. They get angry at God for
not answering their prayers, while all along *they* are the
problem, not God. Many people like this eventually become
bitter against the church and turn their backs on Christianity
altogether. The problem is in our perspective. We don't see
unsettled family quarrels and misunderstandings as sin—but
God does.

Why would God allow such seemingly small things to
hinder our prayers? Even the smallest sin is a stumbling block
to what God has in store for us. We cannot entertain
bitterness, resentment, and criticism and expect God to
answer our prayers—He won't do it. He is not the slightest
bit interested in our prayers when we harbor sin in our
lives, except for our prayers of repentance. We must make
things right horizontally before we can have much impact
vertically.

We Must Check Our Motives

Another reason God does not answer our prayers is because of our wrong motives. "Ye ask, and receive not, because ye ask amiss, that ye may consume it upon your lusts" (James 4:3). In other words, we are often more interested in our desires than we are in glorifying God. Christ said that His work was to glorify the Father (John 17:4). This must be our work as well. We must learn to pray in a fashion that brings more glory to God than to ourselves. We must pray with a spirit of gratitude, thanksgiving, and praise. We must show our appreciation for the many blessings He has so faithfully given us. He has blessed us, not because we deserve it, but because He loves us. At the same time we must commit ourselves to be good stewards of whatever He gives us, including the opportunities that come our way.

It all goes back to God's perspective—we must see the big picture. Any other perspective will center our prayers ultimately around us.

One way to keep a check on your motivation is to stop after a few minutes of prayer and ask yourself, *How did I start this prayer? Did I just jump in and start asking? Or did I start off praising the Lord and showing my gratitude for what He has already done for me?* We must be honest with ourselves and check our motives in regard to every request we make.

We Must Have Unwavering Faith

We have already discussed the fact that God sometimes waits to teach us to trust Him. But many times God cannot answer us because of our lack of faith. All of us have some measure of faith, but many times we go to God with wavering faith. James says, in relation to prayer, "But let him ask in faith, nothing wavering. For he that wavereth is like a wave of the sea driven with the wind and tossed. For let not that man think that he shall receive anything of the Lord" (James 1:6-7).

We may have some initial apprehension about certain requests. But as God confirms His approval through His

Word, the wavering should cease. God uses this initial wavering to test and stretch our faith. But He never intended this to be the normal state of prayer. Wavering faith is not the faith God responds to.

Focus on His Word

We are not to look at what is happening, but at His Word. The Bible is the anchor of our faith. Regardless of what kind of storms come our way, regardless of our circumstances, we are to keep looking at the Word. He wants our prayers to be God-centered, Christ-centered, and Spirit-centered—not thing-centered, trial-centered, and circumstance-centered. For if our prayers are centered on anything other than the Lord, our faith will waver. Why? Because He is the only firm, unchanging foundation on which to base anything, especially our prayers.

All of us have some measure of faith. Often we look at others and envy their faith, thinking that our prayers would be more readily answered if we had their faith. This may be true, but we must keep in mind that God is in the process of building our faith. Each prayer is an opportunity to grow. We must learn to pray for things with our eyes and hearts full of God. We must learn then to wait, disregarding what we see and feel, till God leads us otherwise.

Selfishness Hinders Our Prayers

The next reason God doesn't answer our prayers is because we are stingy. "Whoso stoppeth his ears at the cry of the poor, he also shall cry himself, but shall not be heard" (Prov. 21:13). If we refuse to listen to somebody who has needs, can we expect God to listen to our prayers and meet our needs? That would be an absolute contradiction of Christ's whole message. We cannot turn a deaf ear to someone who is in need because we don't have time or don't want to be bothered, and then expect God to bless us. He doesn't work that way.

For example, can a person who refuses to tithe and give to

the poor or to missionaries expect God to bless him financially? This is hypocrisy. To bless a man such as that would be to encourage him to live in total opposition to what God intends. And besides, anyone who claims to be a Christian and claims that God is meeting all of his needs, and yet will not tithe is a liar.

God uses both our needs and His blessings to teach us to trust Him. But when we become stingy with God's blessings, they stop. When we turn a deaf ear to known needs, our prayers will in no way prompt God to any action on our behalf. We have freely received; we must freely give.

Indifference to God's Word

God will not answer our prayers if we are indifferent to His Word. "He that turneth away his ear from hearing the Law, even his prayer shall be [an] abomination" (Prov. 28:9). God intends for our souls to be "crushed" with a desire for His Word, as the psalmist says (Ps. 119:20, NASB). We should be constantly seeking the deeper truths of Scripture. We weren't left here to be spoon-fed all our lives. God sent the Holy Spirit into each of us so that we may understand for ourselves what God has to say through His Word.

Many Christians have turned their backs on God's Word, either out of lack of understanding or lack of conviction. Others don't mind hearing God's Word, but they make no attempt to understand it or apply it to their lives.

God detests the prayers of a man who has no delight in His Word. When we live with a closed Bible, we live with a closed heaven; God will not answer our prayers.

Unconfessed Sin

The final reason God doesn't answer prayer is unconfessed sin. It must be clear that unconfessed sin short-circuits prayer. Isaiah wrote, "Behold, the Lord's hand is not shortened, that it cannot save; neither His ear heavy, that it cannot hear; but your iniquities have separated between you and your God, and your sins have hid His face from you, that He will not hear" (Isa. 59:1-2). It is not that God *cannot* hear; but He *will* not hear. Our unconfessed sin causes God to turn His back on our prayers and refuse to listen. God will not put a spiritual crowbar into our lives and open us up; He will just wait.

We can pray and pray, but God will not move an inch till we confess our sin. He wants us to voluntarily open our hearts and allow Him to cleanse us. If we are going to pray, we shouldn't waste our time when God isn't listening. And besides, what sin is worth more to us than a relationship with God? Nothing is more valuable than unhindered, two-way communication with Him. In fact, He desires this for us more than we desire it for ourselves.

Now is the time to take each unanswered prayer to the Lord and ask Him why He is not responding. He may point out some sin in your life, or He may refocus your attention on His face. Whatever the situation, don't continue to make excuses for God in regard to your unanswered prayers. In every situation He is seeking to conform you to the image of His Son. As you keep this in mind, you'll pray more in line with God's will—and you'll see more answered prayers.

7
How to Pray in the Will of God

And this is the confidence that we have in Him, that if we ask any thing according to His will, He heareth us: and if we know that He hears us, whatsoever we ask, we know that we have the petitions that we desired of Him.

1 John 5:14-15

How can I know that my prayer request is in keeping with the will of God? How will I know that my petition is pleasing to the Father? Can I be sure that what I am asking is right?

These are among the most legitimate and frequently asked questions about prayer. What is more discouraging than praying when you aren't sure your request is compatible with God's plan?

On the other hand, what greater motivation for prayer can we have than to approach the Father with unwavering confidence that our request has His divine approval?

Some prayer requests need not be sifted through the will of God, for the Bible is unmistakenly clear about some things. We never have to pray: "Lord, save my dad from his life of sin *if it be Thy will.*" Jesus said, "I am come to seek and to save that which is lost" (see Luke 19:10). God "is long-suffering to

73

usward, not willing that any should perish, but that all should come to repentance" (2 Peter 3:9).

Whenever the Bible is specific and clear in its promises, we can pray with confidence. No one ever need pray, "Lord, help me to be forgiving toward those who have wronged me, *if it be Thy will.*" Our Lord makes it very clear as to what our attitude should be toward those who wrong us. "And be ye kind one to another, tender hearted, forgiving one another, even as God for Christ's sake hath forgiven you" (Eph. 4:32).

We do not always have such specific direction about our petitions. Yet He will guide us in our prayers to pray in His will.

When Jesus said, "Ask, and it shall be given you, seek and you shall find, knock and it shall be opened unto you" (Matt. 7:7), He indicated His desire to meet our needs. Paul wrote that we are to "be careful for nothing, but in everything by prayer and supplication with thanksgiving, let your requests be made known to God" (Phil. 4:6). This passage in 1 John 5:14-15 shows us the same truth—God wants us to ask Him to take care of our needs.

At first it seems quite simple. All we have to do is ask, and God gets busy answering our prayers. But there is really more to it than that. God puts conditions on His promises. But these conditions are for our good; they aren't excuses for God not to answer our prayers. "This is the confidence that we have in Him, that if we ask anything according to His will, He heareth us" (1 John 5:14). This is the condition—that we ask according to His will. But how do we know if we are praying in God's will?

Shooting in the Dark

At times all of us feel that our prayers are shooting in the dark. We feel as though a particular request is right at the moment, but when we don't see an immediate answer, we wonder if it was ever God's will to begin with. Our faith decreases instead of increases because we never have any real assurance of what we are praying for. So we shoot in the dark and hope that God will be in agreement and will respond favorably.

This is not the way God wants His people praying. What good would it do for us to pray if we don't have any hint what to pray for? That would be a waste of His time and ours. But His Word gives us clear direction on how to find His will in prayer.

A Threefold Promise

God makes us a threefold promise in 1 John 5:14-15. First, He promises to listen if we pray according to His will. Second, He promises that we already possess what we have asked for. Third, he promises that *we know* that we have the petitions we desire. So when we pray according to His will, He hears us, we have what we ask for, and *we know* that we have what we ask for.

The word *confidence* in verse 14 means boldness or assurance. Among the Greeks this word was used as a political term and referred to the freedom to speak publicly. So as children of God, we can go to Him openly and boldly make our requests. Even the mood of the verb *ask* indicates the idea of making a personal request.

We must forget the notion that we cannot ask anything for ourselves. That is not what the Scriptures teach. These two verses deal with our capacity to approach God openly, freely, confidently, and boldly with the assurance that He will hear and grant what we ask. As a result, we know that we will have what we ask for now.

But now back to this matter of praying in God's will. We say, "Oh, *that's* the catch." And in one sense, it *is* a catch. For many sincere, well-meant prayers have gone unanswered as a result of our praying out of God's will. Can we always know the will of God in our prayers? Yes, although not always at first. Sometimes when we go to God, we are in the dark—we don't know what to ask for. So in the beginning we do not know His will. But if we can understand and apply certain principles, ultimately we can know God's will as we pray.

Stumbling Blocks

Satan throws three stumbling blocks in our way to keep us from finding God's will when we pray. He says, "How can you make a request in faith when you don't know if God is in agreement with you? And if you aren't sure that God agrees with your prayers, why waste your time praying in the first place?"

But if we decide to pray anyway, Satan taunts us. "Look at your past," he says. "You don't have the right to ask God for anything. God isn't going to listen to *you*." At this point, we get our self-esteem mixed up with whether our request is of God. So we either quit praying, or pray and tack onto the end, "if it be Your will."

If we end all our prayers with, "if it be Your will," what do we have? Uncertainty! We don't have any assurance of an answer. This brings us to the passage in the Book of James which says, "Whereas ye know not what shall be on the morrow. For what is your life? It is even a vapor, that appeareth for a little time, and then vanisheth away. For that ye ought to say, 'If the Lord will, we shall live, and do this, or that' " (James 4:14-15). This passage is not referring to prayer, but to presumption in planning for the future.

For some people, Matthew 26:39 is the reason their prayers end with that little phrase. There Jesus was praying in the Garden of Gethsemane. Some say, "Jesus didn't know for sure if He had to die on the cross, so He just left it up to the Father to make the decision." But that isn't what happened. The cup did not symbolize the cross. Jesus knew that He had to die. In Matthew 16:21, He even spoke of His death. So what was the cup He referred to?

Though our minds cannot comprehend it, there has never been a time when Jesus was not alive. When He came to earth, He was God—the same God that has always been, even before the creation of the universe. On earth, Jesus became a man, but He was still God in every way. When He went to the garden, He wasn't afraid to die; the cup of which He spoke was not death, but something far worse for Him. He knew that He would have to bear the sins of the whole world on Himself. He was struggling with the coming separation from His Father.

Scripture shows that Jesus wasn't questioning whether to obey His Father. The issue was whether there was any other way to atone for man's sin besides His separation from the Father. It is impossible for us to conceive of the closeness Jesus has with the Father. In the same way it is impossible for us to understand what He felt in those moments when He knew that He would be banished from the Father's presence. But even in that intense struggle, Christ was committed to obedience: "Not as I will, but as Thou wilt" (Matt. 26:39). Even in those struggling hours He knew exactly what God's will was. God never left His Son to doubt, and in the same way He will never let us doubt when we are sincerely seeking His will.

Sometimes when we aren't sure about God's will we put out a fleece. In a sense, we make a deal with God. We say, "If this happens, then I will do 'A.' But if that happens, then I will do 'B.' " Seeking God's will in this way is a sign of immaturity. This kind of reasoning leaves no room for any real faith and was never intended to be the normal way to discover God's will. So what approach should we take when we aren't sure how to pray?

Paul prayed for the believers in Colosse to "be filled with the knowledge of His will in all wisdom and spiritual understanding"(Col. 1:9). James wrote, "If any man lack wisdom let him ask of God, that giveth to all men liberally, and upbraideth not; and it shall be given him" (James 1:5). What is wisdom? It is seeing things from God's perspective. When we do not know what God thinks about our requests, we have a right to ask Him.

Paul wrote, "Likewise the Spirit also helpeth our infirmities: for we know not what we should pray for as we ought: but the Spirit Himself maketh intercession for us with groanings which cannot be uttered" (Rom. 8:26). The word *infirmities* doesn't mean illnesses; it refers to spiritual weaknesses—our inability to pray from God's perspective. In other words, the Spirit will pray through us when we don't understand what to pray, and at the same time will give us understanding. So when we pray without understanding, we aren't wasting our time as Satan would have us believe. On the contrary, God is honoring our prayers.

As we continue to pray, God will reveal His will to us. Jesus promised, "Howbeit when He, the Spirit of truth is come, He will guide you into all truth" (John 16:13). Part of the Holy Spirit's task is to guide us into the truth of how we should pray. But He can only do this if we are praying. It is essential that we have a desire to pray in accordance with His will; this is the attitude God honors.

How to Begin

So assuming there is no sin in our lives and we really want to know God's mind in our praying, how should we start? First, we must decide if we are asking God to give us something we want, something we need, or some direction in a matter. Second, we should ask God to give us a passage of Scripture that relates in some way to our request—a passage we can meditate on and through which God can speak to us.

Most Christians overlook the place of Scripture in prayer. But the more we saturate our minds with Scripture, the more we will become familiar with God's way. Then it will be easier for us to distinguish His will from our thoughts. God desires that we know Him more than He desires to answer our prayers. God wants to use each prayer as a tool to familiarize us with His ways, His thoughts, and His desires. If we omit His Word in our prayer life, we miss the ultimate blessing of prayer—knowing God.

Ask God to give you a particular promise from Scripture dealing with your request. Make this the anchor of your faith in this area. Hold onto that verse regardless of what happens or how you feel. Live by it, pray by it, and refuse to give in till you have whatever it is God has promised.

Since God wants us to know His will in our prayers, and

since we know that if we are praying according to His will we already have the thing we ask for, the next step is to begin thanking Him. There is no need to keep asking Him to do what we have already asked Him to do once. In the same way, there is no need to beg Him to do what He has already promised to do. Instead, we should thank Him for it. We should thank Him for the wisdom we are going to experience in our prayers. We should thank Him for granting our desires, meeting our needs, and giving us direction.

Then we must wait. Any more asking will show a lack of faith. It is at this point, however, that our faith will be tested the most. We may want to add, "if it be Your will" to our prayers, just in case we misunderstood. This is why basing our prayers on Scripture is so important—it gives us an anchor. God's Word is unchanging truth. It is in the protected harbor of His Word that we bring our faith to rest.

When we go to God, instead of asking, "Lord, please do this and that," let's ask Him to show us how to pray. Let's ask the Holy Spirit to pray through us from beginning to end. Then we can be assured of praying according to His will. We will pray for things we would never think to pray for otherwise. As we pray, God will show us a side of prayer we have never seen.

When our hearts are clean and we have committed ourselves to obey Him, and yet we have not a clue as to what to pray, God takes the responsibility for showing us. He may use Scripture or He may use circumstances. If our request isn't in keeping with His will, He will redirect our attention on Him and we will lose interest in what we were asking for. Regardless of how He shows us, we must believe that He will. Often we will have to wait. But it is during these times of waiting that we begin to really know God.

As we find God's will in our prayers, He confirms it by filling our hearts with the peace of the Holy Spirit. "Be careful for nothing; but in every thing by prayer and supplication with thanksgiving let your requests be made known unto God. And the peace of God, which passeth all understanding, shall keep your hearts and minds through Christ Jesus" (Phil. 4:6-7). We can know without doubt that we are on His track in our prayers. When this is true, we can pray with the assurance that Christ is praying with us to the same end. Peace in our hearts is God's seal of approval on our prayers.

God desires to give us direction in our prayers. He has promised in His Word to do so. Our responsibility is to seek His direction through Scripture. Once we have found His promise to us, we must dig in and wait while thanking Him for what is already ours. For "if God be for us" (Rom. 8:31) in our prayers, who or what can stand against us?

8
A Time to Wait, a Time to Act

But the children of Israel committed a trespass in the accursed thing: for Achan, the son of Carmi, the son of Zabdi, the son of Zerah, of the tribe of Judah, took of the accursed thing: and the anger of the Lord was kindled against the children of Israel. And Joshua sent men from Jericho to Ai, which is beside Bethaven, on the east side of Bethel, and spake unto them, saying, "Go up and view the country." And the men went up and viewed Ai. And they returned to Joshua, and said unto him, "Let not all the people go up; but let about two or three thousand men go up and smite Ai; and make not all the people to labor thither; for they are but few." So there went up thither of the people about three thousand men: and they fled before the men of Ai. And the men of Ai smote of them about thirty and six men: for they chased them from before the gate even unto Shebarim, and smote them in the going down: wherefore the hearts of the people melted, and became as water. And Joshua rent his clothes, and fell to the earth upon his face before the ark of the Lord until the eventide, he and the elders of Israel, and put dust upon their heads. And Joshua said, "Alas, O Lord God, wherefore hast Thou at all brought this people over Jordan, to deliver us into the hand of the Amorites, to destroy us? Would to God we had been content, and dwelt on the other side [of] Jordan! O Lord, what shall I say, when Israel turneth their backs before their enemies! For the Canaanites and all the inhabitants of the land shall hear of it, and shall environ us round, and cut off our name from the earth: and what wilt Thou do unto Thy great name?"

And the Lord said unto Joshua, "Get thee up; wherefore liest thou thus upon thy face? Israel hath sinned, and they have also transgressed My covenant which I commanded them: for they have even taken of the accursed thing, and have also stolen, and dissembled also, and they have put it even among their own stuff. Therefore the children of Israel could not stand before their enemies, but turned their backs before their enemies, because they were accursed: neither will I be with you any more, except ye destroy the accursed from among you. Up, sanctify the people, and say, 'Sanctify yourselves against tomorrow: for thus saith the Lord God of Israel, "There is an accursed thing in the midst of thee, O Israel: thou canst not stand before thine enemies, until ye take away the accursed thing from among you.' "

Joshua 7:1-13

Imagine for a moment that you lost your job. You know God allowed it to happen for a reason, but you aren't sure what that reason is. You know He wants to teach you something, but what is the next step? Should you just sit and do nothing, waiting for God to act? Or should you go out and look for another job?

Sometimes God wants us to wait. But sometimes when a

situation arises, God challenges us to do something. This particular passage in Joshua is an example.

Background

The people of Israel crossed the Jordan River and faced the fortified city of Jericho (Joshua 6). God told Joshua two things. First of all, He promised him that Jericho would fall to the nation of Israel. Then God revealed the military strategy that Joshua was to use. Humanly speaking, this appeared to be the most naive, ridiculous strategy any commander could pursue. Whoever heard of conquering an enemy by marching around their city once a day for seven days, and then on the seventh day marching around it seven times, blowing trumpets, and shouting? But it worked. God was in it.

When God gives directions, they are precise and detailed. He doesn't give us commands and then leave us to figure them out alone. He gave Joshua explicit instructions as to how Jericho should be taken. He told him when to march, how many times the soldiers were to circle the city, when to shout, and when to be quiet. God knew that if He allowed them to talk, they would have probably murmured against Joshua for his unorthodox strategy. So God specifically told Joshua to keep them quiet.

As a result of their obedience, the nation of Israel experienced tremendous victory. Everyone was praising the Lord and shouting "glory" for what God had done. So Joshua, on the basis of that overwhelming victory, sent spies into the next city to be taken. The spies returned, confident that Ai would be a pushover. They told Joshua that only a couple thousand men would be needed to take the city. And why not? After all, look what they had accomplished at Jericho. The truth was *they* didn't do anything at Jericho; *God* did it all.

Because of their previous victory, the Israelites became overconfident and proud. They no longer felt the need to wait for God's directions. Overconfidence is a Satanic trap, and they fell for it.

Calamity struck at Ai because Joshua didn't listen for God's promise and God's strategy; he listened instead to his own cohorts. The soldiers of Ai came rushing out of the city and routed the Israelites, killing 36 men. The Israelites returned home discouraged and disillusioned. "The hearts of the people melted, and became as water" (Joshua 7:5). They were so overwhelmed with fright that they lost all heart for battle.

Joshua's Prayer

So we find Joshua crying out before God. "Joshua rent his clothes, and fell to the earth upon his face before the ark of the Lord until eventide, he and the elders of Israel, and put dust upon their heads" (v. 6). Tearing his clothes was an outward sign of his grief. Falling on his face before the ark was a sign of his humbling himself before the Lord.

So Joshua prayed:

> Alas, O Lord God, wherefore hast Thou at all brought this people over Jordan, to deliver us into the hand of the Amorites, to destroy us? Would to God we had been content, and dwelt on the other side of Jordan! O Lord, what shall I say when Israel turneth their backs before their enemies! For the Canaanites and all the inhabitants of the land shall hear of it, and shall environ us round, and cut off our name from the earth: and what wilt Thou do unto Thy great name? (vv. 7-9)

Joshua's prayer sounded much like the prayers of the Israelites as they wandered in the wilderness. It seems they would have learned to trust God after that experience. But Joshua was repeating the same old lines, "Oh God, why did You allow us to get into this mess? Why didn't You leave us over on the other side of Canaan?"

Joshua didn't mention a single promise from God in his prayer; there was no thanksgiving for the good things God had done and no praise for the Lord either. In fact, his prayer was one of total defeat; this shows what he had his eyes on.

We have all come to God at times with this kind of prayer. We cry out, "Oh Lord, why did You let me get into such a mess? Why do You treat me this way?" We blame God for our unpleasant circumstances. But look what God told Joshua: "Get thee up; wherefore liest thou thus upon thy face?" (v. 10) God had something for Joshua to do; his time for crying was over.

When God sent the men of Israel into Jericho, He told them to kill every man, woman, and child. He also told them that "all the silver, and gold, and vessels of brass and iron, are consecrated unto the Lord: they shall come into the treasury of the Lord" (6:19). What Joshua didn't know was that these instructions concerning the spoils were not followed. God told Joshua that Israel had sinned and that it was his responsibility to rid Israel of "the accursed thing," which they had stolen. It was this sin of covetousness that caused God's wrath to fall on Israel at Ai. So God told Joshua to quit crying and assemble the elders together to find the source of the problem.

Joshua obeyed God and soon found out that Achan was the guilty one. He had taken a Babylonian garment, 200 shekels of silver, and a wedge of gold which was to be offered to God. As a result, Achan and his entire family were stoned and burned. God removed His wrath from Israel and restored His blessing. After that, the Israelites defeated Ai swiftly.

Often we make the mistake in our prayers of talking too much and not listening enough. After we pray about something for a while and nothing happens, or things even get worse, we develop an attitude like Joshua's. We start blaming God, maybe not audibly, but in our own thinking. We look at other people and ask God why He doesn't bless us the same way He blesses them.

Instead of complaining, we need to ask God why we are defeated; then we should be quiet and listen. When we give God the opportunity, He will show us what to do.

A young man came into my office one morning to talk to me about which seminary he should attend. As we talked, I asked him when he felt God called him to the ministry. He said that three years before he felt that God wanted him to preach. He told his wife what he felt God wanted him to do and they were both excited about entering the ministry together.

Soon after that he was given a raise at work. God blessed in other ways as well to aid him in his change of vocation. But instead of immediately following up God's call with some action, he kept praying about it. He said that he knew he should've taken some steps to prepare for the ministry, but he didn't.

Then the blessings ceased and the man felt pressure from God to get on with it. But instead he stalled for three years. Finally the pressure was too much and he headed out to do what he knew God wanted him to do.

There will be times when we come to the Lord with a situation and God will say, "When you correct this relationship, or when you pay this debt, or when you obey Me in this area, then I will bless you." Usually what He shows us has nothing to do with our prayer request. For example, what did one wedge of gold from Jericho have to do with a victory at Ai? In one sense nothing, but in God's eyes it was worth the lives of 36 soldiers. It may be the way you run your business; it may be a habit; or it could be something you do not even consider wrong, but God has told you it has to go.

But in these situations we usually keep on praying. We may even thank God for His forgiveness. We hope that if we pray enough about it, God will let the matter slide. Instead of courageously taking action, we avoid the situation.

But the longer we wait, the longer God withholds His blessings. God is saying to us, "Why don't you quit complaining about your circumstances and get this thing straightened out?" Sometimes we aren't sure what the problem is. But if we honestly allow God to search our hearts, the problem usually becomes evident.

For example, let's say that in your past you borrowed money from someone and did not pay him back. Sometimes in your prayers this debt looms up before you. Your response may be, "Lord, I know You know about that, and I want to thank You for forgiving me." But it keeps coming back. God is trying to say that though you are forgiven, there is still restitution to be made. God is waiting for you to deal with the unpaid debt; then He will restore His hand of blessing on you.

We need to see the big picture, God's big picture. He is not concerned about the money you owe someone or your apologizing to someone for something you may not even remember. But He *is* concerned about your obedience to the initial prompting of His Spirit. He is concerned about how long it takes you to obey Him once you know the truth. Delay is quiet rebellion, and rebellion is sin. To continue praying about something and at the same time refuse to do what you know to be right is covering a rebellious spirit in a cloak of false humility. It is sin (James 4:17).

Importance of Timing
There are five principles in this story of Joshua which we should keep in mind. First, there is a time to wait and a time to act. The time to wait is when we don't know what God wants us to do. The time to act is the moment God shows us what to do and how to go about it.

We Can't Blame God
Second, we should remember that blaming God for our problems is a waste of time. When we find ourselves even slightly shifting the blame to God, it is time for reevaluation. God will allow certain difficulties to surround us, but always with our best interests at heart. When we become critical of our circumstances, we become critical of God. And when we become critical of Him, we are putting more faith in *our* wisdom than in His. This is how we lose sight of God's big picture.

Chuck was losing his business when he came to talk to me

about it. In the course of our conversation, I advised him to read Proverbs and to apply the principles in that book which deal with business. Then we both agreed that he should tithe his income.

About one month later, Chuck came to see me again. His business was booming and everything seemed to be going his way. He was praising the Lord and giving Him all the glory for what had happened.

Three months after that, Chuck's business fell apart again—this time worse than before. He quit going to church, he quit tithing, and he refused to pick up the Bible. According to his wife, Chuck blamed the whole mess on God. Things were worse than ever around the house and there seemed to be no hope for any change.

Then one day in the midst of all the disappointment and heartache, Chuck realized what was happening. He admitted to his wife that the Lord had asked him to give up a certain habit and that he had refused. He said he knew that his problems were his own fault and that he had been wrong in blaming God.

We May Not See a Relationship

Third, we should remember that the thing we need to correct may not even relate to what we are praying about. Since this is true, if we are not honest with ourselves we will conclude, "This does not even relate to my present circumstances. Surely this is not from the Lord." But if the same thing keeps coming up time after time, you can rest assured it *is* from God—regardless of how long ago it happened.

Chuck couldn't see how his financial problem related to his bad habit. But his financial collapse was God's way of getting his attention. When Chuck saw what God was doing, he quit blaming Him and straightened up.

Late Obedience Is Disobedience

Fourth, we must deal with these issues immediately. Late obedience is disobedience. God is not interested in our prayers when we use them to stall Him. If we ask the Lord, He will show us what needs to be done. Not only that, He will give us explicit directions as to how and when to carry them out. But on receiving His directions, we must act.

Blessing Follows Obedience

Fifth, we can expect God's blessing to follow our obedience to His commands. For Israel, the conquest of Ai followed—not preceded—the stoning of Achan. God's blessing is often dependent on our obedience.

Perhaps as you read this chapter God has reminded you of something that you need to deal with. It may relate to your family, your job, or your friends. But whatever it is, God wants you to deal with it because He wants the best for you. When He points out something in your life, it is with a finger of love attached to the hand that bears the mark of that love, a nail print. One of the primary reasons why many of God's people are not greatly blessed of God is because they will not get up off their faces and deal with the attitude or action which God has exposed as disobedience.

Continuous prayer without dealing with the point of divine conflict will cheat us out of the success God desires for us in our prayer life. Nothing is more valuable than an unhindered communication with God the Father. As He shines His searchlight of love into your life, will you deal with the thing He exposes as foreign to His will for your life? Will you deal with it now?

9
Praying for Others

I exhort therefore, that, first of all, supplications, prayers, intercessions, and giving of thanks, be made for all men; for kings, and for all that are in authority; that we may lead a quiet and peaceable life in all godliness and honesty. For this is good and acceptable in the sight of God our Saviour; who will have all men to be saved, and to come unto the knowledge of the truth. For there is one God, and one mediator between God and men, the man Christ Jesus; who gave Himself a ransom for all, to be testified in due time. Whereunto I am ordained a preacher, and an apostle, (I speak the truth in Christ, and lie not;) a teacher of the Gentiles in faith and verity. I will therefore that men pray everywhere, lifting up holy hands, without wrath and doubting.

1 Timothy 2:1-8

All of us have had the frustrating experience of praying for others and seeing no results. We blame it on our lack of faith or on some unknown sin in our lives. But often the real problem is that we aren't aware of what the Bible teaches about praying for others. Scripture makes it clear that when we pray for others certain principles should be followed. It is important that we understand and apply these principles if we are going to see God meet the needs and make the necessary changes in the lives of those for whom we pray. But let's take a close look at the people the Bible instructs us to pray for.

Those in Authority
Paul says that we are to pray for kings and all those in authority (1 Tim. 2:2). For us that would mean our President, our congress, our mayor, and even our boss. We are to intercede in their behalf, taking their needs to the Lord. Then we are to give thanks for them.

The moral decline in America, corruption in high places, loss of credibility among our leaders, and loss of faith in them by the citizens require renewed commitment on our part to pray for our leaders.

We should pray that every person who runs for public office as well as those appointed, would fear God and acknowledge Him as Lord. With ungodly men in authority, how can we "lead a quiet and peaceable life in all godliness and honesty"? (v. 2) Ungodly leadership creates conflict and strife. The writer of Proverbs declares, "When the righteous are in authority, the people rejoice: but when the wicked bear rule, the people mourn" (Prov. 29:2).

Paul exhorts us to pray (1 Tim. 2:1). This word *exhort* means to encourage strongly. We are strongly encouraged to pray for the men and women in public office. We should pray that they might see the problems that plague our society from God's point of view. If ever there was an admonition that needs to be heeded by God's people, it is this word from Paul to pray for those in authority.

The Body of Christ
Next we are to pray for the body of Christ—the church. We are responsible for praying for all the saints (Eph. 6:18). One part of the body of Christ is under persecution. Another part

is lukewarm. Another part is cold, having set aside the truth of the Word of God and doubting its authenticity. Still another part of the body is in financial need. We are to intercede for each part according to its specific needs, not just toss out a general request such as, "Bless the church." We are to pray for *all* the saints, not just the group we are personally involved with.

Vocational Servants

We should also pray for God's servants—those who have been called into full-time service. In a sense, we are all full-time servants. But we should particularly pray for those who have made spiritual service their life vocations—pastors, teachers, missionaries, and evangelists.

Paul tells us how. First, we are to pray that utterance would be given; that is, we are to pray that God would show His servants what to preach and teach. Second, we are to pray that these special servants would speak the truth boldly. Then we are to pray that they would make known the mystery of the Gospel—that their message would be clear. These are three specifics Paul knew from personal experience to be the keys to an effective ministry.

As a pastor, there is nothing more reassuring than to know that people are praying for me. There is an elderly, semi-invalid preacher in our church who gets up at 2:00 every morning to pray for me. Occasionally he sends me verses dealing with the specific needs the Lord has laid on his heart concerning my life. He is always right on target and his letters and verses are always an encouragement.

For pastors, no asset is more precious than the consistent prayers of God's people. However, one major problem in the church today is that people spend more time *criticizing* their pastor than they do *praying* for him. More than ever, God's servants need to be upheld in prayer. More than ever they need utterance, boldness, and clarity in presenting the Gospel. It is time we stopped criticizing and started interceding.

Laborers

Next we are to pray for the laborers, the people yet to be called. Jesus challenged His disciples, "Pray ye therefore the Lord of the harvest, that He will send forth laborers into His harvest" (Matt. 9:38). We are to pray for those whom God calls to heed His call and go forth in His power preaching, teaching, singing, and taking places of leadership in the church.

There are people at this very moment struggling with God's call to enter the ministry. The enemy is doing all in his power to draw them into the world. These people need our prayers, especially to bind Satan's powers from influencing their decision. We need to pray that they would be sensitive and obedient to the promptings of the Spirit.

The Lost

Likewise, we are to pray for the lost. The vast majority of Scriptures relating to prayer admonish us to pray for the saints. But Paul also tells us that it is God's will for everyone to be saved (1 Tim. 2:4-6). To pray for the lost is to pray in accordance with God's will.

Our Enemies

There is one last group we are to pray for—our enemies. Jesus said, "Love your enemies, bless them that curse you, do good to them that hate you, and pray for them which despitefully use you and persecute you" (Matt. 5:44). If is often difficult to pray for those we don't like, especially if they feel the same way toward us. So why are we instructed to pray for our enemies? For the same reason we are to pray for everyone else: in order "that we may lead a quiet and peaceable life in all godliness and honesty" (1 Tim. 2:1). The point is this: none of these prayers are to be based on personal likes or dislikes, but rather on our desire for peace and godliness for all mankind.

One result of placing godly men in office and praying for them is a peaceful and godly society. In the same way, praying for our authority at home or work will result in peace in those places. God may bring peace by first working in us, but regardless of how He does it, He promises the end result will be the same.

Through prayer God closes gaps created by conflict. Then He manifests His Spirit of godliness and reverence. Peace and godliness in our homes, our nation, and our jobs depend on our prayers. I am convinced that if God's people will pray the way God intended, He will work a miracle in this country. There will be a quietness and peace this generation has never known.

But if we fail to pray, our society will continue to spiral downward into chaos. God's people are responsible. For only we have access to Almighty God—the Source of power who is able to change this degenerating condition.

How to Pray

Now that we understand who we are to pray for, let's find out how to pray for them. Too often we pray for others to appease our consciences, and not with the intent or expectation of change. We pray vague prayers with no specific blessings in mind. If we are going to pray, let's learn to pray effectively.

A Heart of Compassion

We must keep in mind that we are to pray from hearts of love and compassion. Prayers that have the slightest hint of prejudice or anger will not be heard by God. And besides, we will not pray consistently for people toward whom we feel resentment and bitterness. Regardless of what was done or who was to blame, God wants our attitudes right when we pray.

We are not to live our lives reacting to others, but rather responding to His Spirit. If we are willing for God to heal our bitterness toward our enemies, He will do it; many times He will do it through our prayers for them. But whatever the case, we must pray from hearts filled with love and compassion.

Prayer Is the Link

Next we must realize that our prayers are the link between God's inexhaustible resources and people's needs. Through prayer we direct God's hand of infinite resources to the hand of the person in need. God is the source of power, but we are the instrument He uses to link the two together. We stand in the gap between the need and the satisfaction of that need. When we see ourselves in that position, we will understand the need for consistent unwavering prayer. We will begin to pray without ceasing.

One afternoon a pastor from another city came by seeking advice about a church problem. A few deacons in his church were trying to run things. They were a real source of irritation and this pastor had taken as much as he could stand. That evening his church was going to discuss the manner in which deacons were to be selected. These particular men had threatened to challenge the pastor publicly before the whole congregation. They had been successful in getting their way till then and this pastor knew that it was time to turn things around or the church would really suffer.

He was troubled and fearful. We talked for a while and I gave him a verse to claim during the business meeting. "I will go in the strength of the Lord God: I will make mention of Thy righteousness, even of Thine only" (Ps. 71:16). Then I told him I would pray. I stood in the gap between the pastor and the victory he needed. I prayed specifically that God would close the mouths of those who would come against my friend as God closed the mouths of the lions in Daniel's case.

Late that night he called me back. He was so excited I could hardly understand him. He said that it was the smoothest business meeting they had ever had and that nobody said a word in opposition to his proposals.

Sometimes we will be the only person standing in the gap in a given situation. This is especially true if we are the only person that knows of a particular need. Intercession in this case becomes our sole responsibility. This kind of prayer is work, yet it is rewarding. This is how Christ prayed, for He stood in the gap between God and all mankind. He was the link between God and the whole human race. In the same way, we must make ourselves available for the sake of others.

Identify with Their Needs

To pray effectively for others we must be able to identify with their needs. Spiritually and emotionally, we must feel what they feel. When Jesus looked out over the crowd, He had "compassion for them" (Matt. 20:34; also see 9:36; 14:14; Mark 1:41; Luke 7:13). He felt what they felt. Christ was tempted and tried in every point that we are (Heb. 4:15). Why? One reason was so He could pray effectively for us. He knows how we feel in every situation we face. When you and I talk with the Lord He can identify with us. He lived at home for 30 years; He knows the problems encountered there. He worked in a carpenter's shop; He can identify with the laborer. He was hated and rejected; He can identify with the downtrodden.

I was able to identify with the pastor who faced the opposition in his church because I had faced a similar situation. As I prayed, I remembered how I had felt when I faced opposition from deacons. I remembered the feelings of rejection. I remembered the pressure I felt every Sunday as I stood to preach. All of this motivated me to pray earnestly for my friend. Identifying with him allowed me to pray in a way that few other people could pray.

Purpose for Suffering

One primary reason God allows us to suffer is so we can identify with others in our prayers. Until we suffer, we tend to stereotype those who suffer as inferior and weak. We have little patience with them, much less any burden to pray for them. But Christ lived among the rejected and suffering. He was one of them.

When we avoid pain, we limit our usefulness to God. Through the comfort we receive in our trials, we learn to comfort others (2 Cor. 1:4). This verse implies that if we have never needed comforting, we won't know how to comfort others.

So if we are going to pray for others, we must ask the Lord to help us see what others see, and feel what they feel. We must understand their hurts. And the only way to do that is to experience hurt ourselves. When we share in another's pain, we will pray with an earnestness we have never known before.

Desire the Best for Others

As we pray for others, we must desire their highest good. We must die to all selfish desires concerning them and seek only God's best. We can put no conditions on God in our prayers—no matter what the cost to us. For example, if a girl is praying for her boyfriend to be saved, she must be willing to do anything for God to answer her prayer. If she says, "I'll do anything but break up with him," then God may only answer her prayer on the condition that she become willing to break up. When we give God a condition, He often makes *that* the condition on which the answer to our prayer hinges.

Carl had been praying for months about his rebellious son. His 22-year-old son had left home and was living with some boys in a shack outside of town. My friend knew his son had been involved with drugs before he left home and soon after learned that his son had become a drug dealer. Carl's two main concerns were that God would bring his son home and that his son wouldn't be arrested.

One morning while he was praying for his son, God spoke to Carl. Carl realized that his had been a selfish request. He was well known in his town and would be embarrassed if his son were arrested on drug charges. Carl told the Lord that if the only way to deliver his son from his sin was to allow him to be arrested then he was willing for that to happen—even at the expense of his reputation.

A few days later, Carl received a phone call from the police. His son had been arrested and was charged with possession of illegal drugs. As Carl drove to the police station to pick up his son, he realized that God had been waiting for him to get his attitude right before He could allow his son to come home.

God honored Carl's obedience. He and his son rebuilt their broken relationship and soon afterward his son left home again, this time to study for the ministry.

When we pray for someone we must take our hands off the matter completely and let God work *any* way He sees fit. It may not come out the way we want it, but the outcome will always be in the best interest of both parties.

Being Part of the Answer

When praying for others, we must be willing to be part of the answer if necessary. If we aren't willing to be used to answer our own prayers, we aren't cooperating with God. As a result, He won't cooperate with us; He won't answer our prayers. Why? Because these are prayers of isolation and separation. We are saying, "God, I don't want to get mixed up in anyone's problems. *You* take care of that."

Can you imagine Jesus doing that? "Sorry, Bartimaeus, I don't want to get *My* hands dirty." God will not hear our prayers of isolation. If we aren't more interested than that, then He's not interested in our prayers. As long as we ask and do nothing, He will listen and do nothing. If it costs us nothing, we can expect little in return.

Don't pray for more missionaries unless you're willing to go yourself or are willing to send your children. Don't pray for another's financial need unless you're willing to give yourself. And don't pray for the lost unless you're willing to go to them and share what Christ means to you.

We Must Persevere

When we intercede for others, we must persevere. We must be willing to keep on praying till the answer comes. One reason we don't see more answers to prayer is because we aren't willing to pay the price; and often the price is *time*. If we are really burdened for someone and are really feeling what they feel, we can't possibly stop praying till their burden is lifted. But if we are only praying out of pity or to appease our consciences, we will soon forget the one in need. One true test of loyalty to our friends is if we are willing to lay down our lives for them in prayer. Our faithfulness to our friends can be measured by the consistency of our prayers for them.

We lie when we flippantly say to people, "I love you," and then forget to pray for them in their time of need. Yet how many times has someone asked us to pray about a specific need and we say, "I'll be praying for you"—then we pray for them casually, if we remember them at all. We need to examine ourselves and see if we really know what love is all about. We pray consistently for those we really love. This is the reason our prayers are so often full of our own desires and needs.

Ask God to show you three people He wants you to pray for—three people who have burdens, heartaches, or specific needs. Tell God you are willing to be part of the answer. Then ask Him to share their burden with you. Ask God for a real spirit of compassion and love for these three. Tell Him you want Him to teach you how to pray and intercede on their behalf. Start with three and then add as the Lord leads.

If all of us were to start praying for each other, the Spirit of God would release the blessing of heaven on us. Homes would be mended, businesses would be blessed, and churches would be in a constant spirit of revival. There is no way to describe what God would do in your own life if you would apply these simple principles to your prayers. But you will never *be* the same nor *pray* the same again.

10
Prayer Is Where the Action Is

Then came Amalek, and fought with Israel in Rephidim. And Moses said unto Joshua, "Choose us out men, and go out, fight with Amalek: tomorrow I will stand on the top of the hill with the rod of God in mine hand." So Joshua did as Moses had said to him, and fought with Amalek: and Moses, Aaron, and Hur went up to the top of the hill. And it came to pass, when Moses held up his hand, that Israel prevailed: and when he let down his hand, Amalek prevailed. But Moses' hands were heavy; and they took a stone, and put it under him, and he sat thereon; and Aaron and Hur stayed up his hands, the one on the one side, and the other on the other side; and his hands were steady until the going down of the sun. And Joshua discomfited Amalek and his people with the edge of the sword.

Exodus 17:8-13

As the children of Israel traveled through the wilderness on their way to Canaan, many who were weak and sick fell to the rear of the caravan and were left to keep up the best way they could. As a result, the Israelites were stretched out many miles through the desert. Amalek, a nomadic tribe of that region, took advantage of this situation and attacked and plundered those who fell behind. So the Israelites were forced to fight even though they were far less prepared for war than the Amalekites. It was no secret that the Israelites had walked out of Egypt loaded down with as much wealth as they could carry. The Amalekites were willing to take any risk to steal this wealth for themselves.

Moses tells Joshua to choose his men and fight the Amalekites (Ex. 17:9). In the meantime Moses, Aaron, and Hur climbed a hill where they could watch the battle. As the two armies began fighting, Moses raised the rod of God above his head and there was an immediate turn in the battle; the nation of Israel began to win. When he lowered the rod because of weariness, Amalek began winning the battle. It quickly became apparent to Moses, Aaron, and Hur that the determining factor in this battle was whether or not Moses held his staff up. So Aaron and Hur sat Moses on a rock and each one of them took one of Moses' arms and held it up. And even though the army of Israel was at a disadvantage because of their lack of equipment and preparation, they still defeated the Amalekites.

Where the Battle Is Won

The battle wasn't won because of the army's strength or because of Joshua's military genius. The battle was won on the hilltop as Aaron and Hur held up the hands of Moses. It was the action on the hilltop that determined the outcome of the action in the valley.

There are three principles found in this incident which, if observed carefully, will make our prayer lives more exciting and our prayers more fruitful. First, life's battles are won or lost in the place of prayer, not on the battlefield of everyday life. The real spiritual success or failure of a church does not depend on the talent of the preacher, the size of the congregation, or the strength of the organization. Success from God's point of view will only be obtained through prayer. The person who sees these other things as the criteria for success has no concept of the working of the Holy Spirit. It is by these outward signs that the world judges the church. But God does not win His battles through outward signs. God wins His battles through men and women who intercede on behalf of the kingdom.

There was a time when I dreaded our monthly deacons' meetings. They usually lasted for over three hours, and when we finished I was drained emotionally and physically because so little was usually accomplished. Then the Lord laid it on one of the deacon's hearts to begin a Saturday morning prayer meeting for the deacons.

Each Saturday we met and prayed for two or three hours. The Lord began to knit our hearts together in an unusual way. There was a oneness of mind and purpose among us like there had never been before.

Soon the nature of our monthly meetings changed. The atmosphere was more relaxed and everyone was more agreeable. The meeting time was cut to less than half of what it was before, and everyone agreed that we accomplished more. Business was taken care of so quickly that we moved the meeting time to Sunday afternoon.

The deacons agreed that praying together on Saturday morning made the difference. God's business, for the most part, is to be taken care of on our knees. When dealing with any situation, first we must pray. For it is on our knees that the real work is done.

In this incident from the Book of Exodus, God wanted to teach Moses, Joshua, and the rest of the people a lesson. There was more going on than just a battle between two armies. A great spiritual battle was going on as well. God's message was this: in our spiritual conflicts the outcome is not determined by what is seen in the field of battle, but rather by what happens in the place of prayer. That is why throughout the Old Testament God put His people in arenas where they faced overwhelming disadvantages. Then to the amazement of all who saw or heard, His people proved victorious. Why?

Because out of a spirit of total dependence on Him and unwavering faith in Him they fought the real battles on their faces before God. Their public victories were the outcome of their private victories.

As we, in total dependence on God, bow our knees before the conflict begins, God turns our eyes toward Him. He sifts and cleanses us in preparation for the coming battle. God gives us His perspective of the battle, which is always far superior to our own. Our faith soars as we see that those who war against us must also war against the Christ who is within us. He shows us His sufficiency for whatever we are facing. Then He promises us victory by His own Word. As we rise from our places of prayer, we march into any battle confident of victory. For the battle is the Lord's and the victory is ours. "Now thanks be unto God, which always causeth us to triumph in Christ" (2 Cor. 2:14).

Many conflicts in the home would be brought to quick conclusions if family members would bow before God, search their own hearts, and surrender the battles to Him. We must realize that He alone is the source of *all* things, spiritual and material (2 Peter 1:3). We must enter into each situation with our total dependence on Him. Then, and only then, will God release His supernatural power to overcome the enemy.

A Lesson Worth Sharing

The lesson Moses learned was so important that God specifically told him to tell Joshua the whole story in detail. God knew that Joshua would soon become the leader of the Israelites. He also knew that through the many battles to be fought, Joshua would need the assurance that God was fighting beside them. God wanted Joshua's perspective of war to be a heavenly perspective. The same must be true for us.

One problem is that we often don't know who the enemy is. We act as if people are our enemies—our families, our bosses, even our friends. But the Bible makes it clear that Satan is our enemy (Eph. 6:12). Satan knew that the Messiah would come through the nation of Israel. The Amalekites and all the other nations that warred with Israel were instruments of Satan—weapons to get at God's people and, in a sense, to get at God.

For the Israelites, the physical conflict was not the real conflict at all. The same is true for conflicts we face. If we don't fight our battles on our knees, we will mistake all kinds of people for the enemy. While they *appear* to be our enemies, Satan is the ultimate source of our conflicts.

A college student was having trouble getting along with her unsaved father. Regardless of how sweet she was, they just could not get along. She soon found herself becoming bitter. As she prayed, the Lord revealed a strategy to combat her bitterness.

She was to understand that the conflict wasn't between her and her father, but rather between Satan and the Christ in her. She saw that Satan was using her father as an instrument to overcome the Christ in her.

When she adopted this attitude, things at home began to change. She no longer saw her father as her enemy. On the contrary, she saw for the first time how he really loved her. When conflicts would arise, instead of reacting to her father, she would go to her knees in prayer and deal with the real enemy.

As Satan sows seeds of disunity throughout the church, many of God's people find themselves in conflict with each other. These conflicts are usually never resolved because nobody deals with the real enemy—Satan. There is no way to win a battle if we don't know who our enemy is. And because our real enemy is a spiritual being, the only way we can really deal with him is on our knees.

God is the source of all our victory. Through faith in Him and His willingness to fight our battles for us, we can approach life from a standpoint of victory regardless of the circumstances. This is not a victory claimed and won on the battlefield of life, but a victory claimed and won on our knees in private before the public battle ever begins.

We May Become Weary

Second we need to remember that when we face life's battles, we will become weary at times. Even Moses, God's greatest statesman, grew weary as he held the rod of God over his head. Though he started out strong, he soon tired and finally dropped his arms completely. He knew that the raised rod was the key to victory, but he just couldn't keep it up. Just in time, Aaron and Hur sat him down and lifted his arms till the battle was over and the Amalekites were defeated.

In spite of the fact that Jesus told us to pray and not faint (Luke 18:1), we still faint. We lose heart. Sometimes it is because we look at the circumstances around us. Other times we just lose the burden. Sometimes Satan warps our perspective to discourage us; we see problems as larger than they really are.

God knows we will grow fainthearted at times. He knows that sometimes we just won't feel like it. He understands when we feel like giving up. But this is where the third principle from this story fits in.

Finding Our Own Aaron and Hur

God sent Moses up to that hill knowing that he couldn't hold the rod up long by himself. It was no accident that Aaron and Hur went along. They gave Moses the support he needed.

In the same way, God won't let us be totally independent of others. God has built His church on a system of interdependence, each person ministering to others through their different talents, gifts, abilities, and prayers. But at the same time, everyone recognizes God as the Source of all blessings.

All of us need an Aaron and a Hur: two people we can share our needs and burdens with. Christ in the Garden of Gethsemane revealed His burden. He too needed the prayer support of His friends, but He found them asleep.

Aaron and Hur didn't serve as Moses' counselors. They didn't tell him how to hold the rod so he wouldn't get tired. They were his supporters. They really held up the rod by supporting Moses' arms.

All too often people will give us advice for our spiritual battles, but they won't give of their time in prayer. Who is willing to listen attentively to your hurts and then to pray till God lifts the burden? We need less counseling and more praying. For God is moved by Spirit-filled praying, not by good advice. And God is the only One with power enough to win our battles for us.

Threefold Cord

"A threefold cord is not quickly broken" (Ecc. 4:12). Something supernatural takes place when three believers with genuine concern for one another and unwavering faith in God intercede for one another. God has honored this type of intercession in my life many times. I have an "Aaron" and a "Hur" who have prayed with me through financial difficulties, family problems, church-related problems, and deep personal hurts. To have two other men get under my burdens with tears in my behalf is one of the most encouraging and strengthening experiences of my spiritual life. It serves as a physical reassurance that God is concerned about my problems. My faith soars in the midst of conflict when I hear the faith-filled prayers of my friends petitioning God on my behalf. And not only does it build my faith, but theirs as well.

For there will be times when we have the opportunity to intercede on behalf of the ones who have prayed for us. As love develops between prayer partners, sensitivity to each others' needs also develops. We recognize and feel their hurts without them saying anything; the Spirit reveals to us who needs prayer. When we have two encouraging forces, our fainteartedness turns into courage and confidence, and God's power becomes a reality.

Spiritually Minded

What kind of people should we look for when we ask God to send us an Aaron and a Hur? First we should look for those who are *spiritually minded* and actively seeking God; those who obey and trust the Lord regardless of the circumstances.

Whether or not we think they are as spiritual as we are is not an issue here. It is the condition of their hearts that matters.

Warriors—Not Counselors. Secondly, we should look for those who accept us as we are, regardless of the problems we may be facing. They must see themselves as sent to lift us up, not criticize us. They must see themselves as prayer warriors, not counselors.

A Compassionate Heart. An Aaron and a Hur must have compassionate hearts. They must be able to feel what we feel. They need to know what it means to hurt. They must also have a willingness to give of themselves and ask nothing in return—to love us as Christ does, unconditionally and unselfishly.

Faithful. Last of all, our prayer warriors must be faithful. We don't need people who will only come when it is convenient. These people must be willing to come when we need them. They must be willing to stop whatever they are doing and come to our aid in prayer. Something happens in our lives when we have an Aaron and a Hur standing by our sides, beseeching Almighty God in our behalf. There is a new freedom and confidence and also greater spiritual fruitfulness. We must ask ourselves: *Am I the kind of Christian that someone would want as an Aaron or a Hur? Do I meet the qualifications?*

There is no way for three people to bind themselves together in Christ and pray for one another without growing and becoming stronger in their faith. Among groups like this the real battles in life are fought and won. This is how God intends for all of us to fight our battles—on our faces before Him with others who will pay any price for victory.

What would happen in our families if we became the Aaron or Hur for our spouses and children? What would happen in our churches and in our businesses if we began praying with people there in the spirit of an Aaron and a Hur? God must strip us of our pride. He is not going to let us make it alone. He wants us to recognize our need for each other and unite spiritually.

What About You?

Are you like the nation of Israel—trapped in a valley and facing battles that time after time defeat you? Then you need an Aaron and a Hur. Ask God to develop in you the needed qualities. Then ask Him to send you two others who likewise have prepared themselves for spiritual battles. A threefold cord is not easily broken, and neither is the faith of three people commited to interceding for one another in the Spirit's power.

11
The
Warfare
of Prayer

Then was brought unto Him one possessed with a devil, blind, and dumb: and He healed him, insomuch that the blind and dumb both spake and saw. And all the people were amazed and said, "Is not this the Son of David?" But when the Pharisees heard it, they said, "This fellow doth not cast out devils, but by Beelzebub the prince of devils." And Jesus knew their thoughts, and said unto them, "Every kingdom divided against itself is brought to desolation; and every city or house divided against itself shall not stand: and if Satan cast out Satan, he is divided against himself; how shall then his kingdom stand? And if I by Beelzebub cast out devils, by whom do your children cast them out? Therefore they shall be your judges. But if I cast out devils by the Spirit of God, then the kingdom of God is come unto you. Or else how can one enter into a strong man's house, and spoil his goods, except he first bind the strong man? And then he will spoil his house. He that is not with Me is against Me; and he that gathereth not with Me scattereth abroad."

Matthew 12:22-30

There is one primary reason we pray weak prayers: we don't comprehend God's promises concerning the release of His supernatural power through prayer. We see prayer as only involving God and our request, and we miss the big picture.

Paul described what warfare prayer is all about when he wrote, "Finally, my brethren, be strong in the Lord, and in the power of His might. Put on the whole armor of God, that ye may be able to stand against the wiles of the devil" (Eph. 6:10-11). We are entering a war where we will need strength greater than our own. He identifies our enemy, Satan, and commands us to make provision to battle against him by putting on the armor of God.

Then Paul stated the realm and nature of warfare prayer: "For we wrestle not against flesh and blood, but against principalities, against powers, against the rulers of the darkness of this world, against spiritual wickedness in high places" (v. 12).

The Enemy We Face Today

The body of Christ is in constant conflict against spiritual forces. When the church of Jesus Christ was born, it was born in the midst of the heathen empire of Rome. Two thousand years later, in America, the church of the Lord Jesus Christ is again in the midst of a heathen empire. It is a capitalistic empire that is anti-God; it is a system whose religion is humanism. Its philosophy declares that man is sufficient within himself to meet his own needs. The church is surrounded by a system that denies there is a God. Man is his own god.

In the early days, the New Testament church suffered persecution for the truth. As a result, the Roman Empire recognized that the Gospel of Jesus Christ was a greater power than the Roman military machine. Christians showed their spiritual power—they believed, they stood, they gave, and they died. And where is the Roman Empire today? For long after the nation of Rome collapsed, the Christian faith continues.

The Challenge

Today in America the body of Christ faces the challenge of humanism. We must decide now if we are going to compromise. Will we close the Word of God? Or will we stand true to what we know is right? Are we willing to pay the price in the 20th century for the sake of future generations?

God knew the enemy we would face, and He did not leave us to fight alone. Through the power of prayer, He has equipped us to overcome the forces and influences of humanism. He has given us the power and responsibility to make an indelible impression on our society. But are we willing to do so?

Prayer has always been our most powerful weapon. And yet we as Christians have allowed our nation to degenerate into its present condition by our failure to exercise our divinely given authority to pray. Yes, we are responsible! Why? Because America has a spiritual problem, and therefore it will take a spiritual answer to solve it.

The Responsibility of the Church

The church has a ministry not only of winning people to Christ, but of dealing with all kinds of people, wherever they are spiritually. We combat Satan to rescue people from his bondage and free them to become the men and women God wants them to be. But because of our weakness and lack of faith, the church has recoiled from such warfare. We have concluded that our only task is to lead people to Christ and put them on the church roll, but that is far from the total purpose of the church.

There are those who say we are not to get involved with political issues or healing, or anything out of the ordinary. Some people teach that healing and casting out demons and many other works of the Holy Spirit ended in the first century. But the responsibility of the body of Christ today is the same as it was 2,000 years ago.

Christ said, "Behold, I give unto you power to tread on serpents and scorpions, and over all the power of the enemy:

and nothing shall by any means hurt you" (Luke 10:19). The first reference to the word power means authority. The second reference means strength. Christ was telling His disciples that He was giving them all the power and strength they needed to overcome all the power and strength of the enemy.

Equipped for the Task

If Christ has given us a responsibility today equal to the responsibility of Christians 2,000 years ago, it only makes sense that He has equipped us with the same power for the task. We have been saved and are being sanctified for the purpose of glorifying God. To glorify Him, we must obey Him. To obey Him, we must take to heart the Great Commission—Go!

Every believer is to carry out Christ's commission in whatever way possible. For 2,000 years, men and women have been going out as a result of Christ's command. We are the fruits of their labors. Each of us has the same responsibility.

God has given the present-day church the same amount of authority and power over satanic forces as He did the first-century church. Since this is true, then we have the same responsibility as the early church to bind the prince of this earth, and reclaim for God what is rightfully His.

There is only one omnipotent Being on the earth, and that is God. Satan is *not* omnipotent; he is merely a fallen angel. But the church acts as if Satan is omnipotent. We treat Satan as if he has equal power with God. We often think of him as just a little less powerful than God. We continue to retreat while Satan advances.

Through Christ, God made His major attack against Satan. Christ's death and resurrection gave us victory over the consequences and the power of sin. Through Christ, we have overcome Satan; he has been conquered. Now God sends us, indwelt by His Spirit and supernaturally endowed, to conquer Satan. We are to reclaim for God the lives of men and women who are in bondage to sin. We are God's ambassadors to a lost and dying world (2 Cor. 5:20).

But we will only accomplish this great work when we get our eyes off our past failures and set them on God and His Word. We must begin to appropriate what is ours, instead of allowing the supernatural power of God to lie dormant within us.

Once some Pharisees were accusing Jesus of casting out demons in the name of Satan (Matt. 12:24). So Christ said, "Look, do you think Satan would cast out his own demonic powers and divide his own kingdom? If I am casting out demons in the name of God, then the kingdom of God has come to your doorsteps, and you do not even recognize it." (See vv. 26-28.) This was the worst accusation Jesus could have made, seeing them as the very ones who were to identify the Messiah when He came.

The Essence of Spiritual Warfare

Jesus summed up the essence of spiritual warfare by saying, "Or else how can one enter into a strong man's house, and spoil his goods, except he first bind the strong man? And then he will spoil his house" (v. 29). Christ again mentioned this idea of binding: "I will give unto thee the keys of the kingdom of heaven: and whatsoever thou shalt bind on earth shall be bound in heaven: and whatsoever thou shalt loose on earth shall be loosed in heaven" (16:19). Spiritual warfare is binding and loosing according to the leading of the Holy Spirit.

We are living in conflict with the world, a conflict that will continue till Jesus comes. We are all involved in one way or another whether we like it or not. We will either be an asset or a hindrance to the army of God; we will either be a victor or a captive.

Paul makes it clear that we are not coming against people or circumstances in this war, for Satan and his host are our enemy (Eph. 6:11-12). This is a spiritual conflict and therefore we must be spiritually prepared. We must have on the *whole* armor of God. And if we are going to put it on we must understand what it is.

Loins Girded with Truth

First we are to have our loins girded with truth. This means more than just reading the Word; we must understand exactly what it says and who it says we are. We must understand our position in Christ and His position in us. By faith we must see that the battleground is in the heavenlies—the real struggle is between God and Satan.

The holes in our theology are where Satan builds his strongholds. Our wrong perspective of spiritual things often leaves us ineffective when it comes to warfare prayer. *Having* the truth is not enough. We must *know* the truth if we are to be set free (John 8:32). We must have our loins girded about with the knowledge and application of the truth if we are to be truly prepared for battle.

The Breastplate of Righteousness

Next we are to wear the breastplate of righteousness. This doesn't mean righteous acts. Instead it means that we are to accept God's gift of righteousness (Rom 5:17). We have already been made the righteousness of God in Christ (2 Cor. 5:21). To be prepared for battle, we must accept that gift of righteousness.

This is hard for most people to do. We aren't taught to think of ourselves as righteous. But it all goes back to the first piece of armor—we must know the truth of God's Word if we are to enter into warfare prayer. When our doctrine is biblically correct, we'll think of ourselves from God's perspective.

The church I attended as a young boy emphasized man's sinfulness. The preacher never mentioned the righteousness we receive when we become Christians. As a result, I grew up feeling condemned by God. I never felt that I could live up to God's expectations of me. This negative teaching made such an impact on me that I spent the first years of my ministry trying to make myself acceptable in God's sight. What a relief it was when I found out that I was acceptable to God just because I was in Christ. I no longer had to worry about what God was thinking about me. In His sight I was righteous. My only responsibility was to accept His gift of righteousness.

The Bible clearly teaches that in Christ we are righteous. To think of ourselves as anything less is to go into battle without the most important part of our armor—the breastplate. Our wrong thinking in this area allows Satan to make us feel unworthy in God's presence. "Who are you to expect God to answer your prayer?" he asks. There is only one answer, "I am the righteousness of God in Christ, that's who I am!" (See 2 Cor. 5:21.)

If God didn't make us as righteous as Christ, how could we get into heaven? Too often we go into battle unprepared. As a result, we neglect our relationship with God because we feel so defeated and so unworthy. We must accept God's gift of righteousness as we enter into spiritual warfare.

The Preparation of the Gospel of Peace

It is essential that we have our feet prepared with the Gospel of peace. The key here is the word *peace*. Paul was referring to the peace we can have in this life. Most of the time we think of the Gospel as the promise of heaven if a person accepts Christ as their Saviour. But Paul was talking about a new life on this earth as a result of accepting Christ. In other words, we must be prepared to lead others to Christ. The person who enters into warfare prayer must understand the peace that God has provided for us on this earth.

Paul wrote, "I am crucified with Christ: nevertheless I live; yet not I, but Christ liveth in me: and the life which I now live in the flesh I live by the faith of the Son of God, who loved me, and gave Himself for me" (Gal. 2:20). This must be a daily experience for real prayer warriors. For peace only comes as we allow Christ to live through us.

This is the side of the Gospel our world needs to see. They have *heard* about heaven: it is time they *see* heaven in our homes, our churches, and our offices. People seek wealth because they see the lifestyle of the wealthy, and people seek Christ when they see the true scriptural lifestyle of Christians. When they come, we must be prepared to guide them into this new life in Christ. We must be prepared to be a part of the answer to our prayers for the lost and backslidden.

The Shield of Faith

Then Paul says we are to take the shield of faith. With this piece of armor we are to quench Satan's fiery darts. Every evil that comes against us is from one source—Satan. We must never lose sight of this; otherwise we will see the instruments of Satan as our enemies and will never deal with him, the root of the problem.

But how does faith defeat Satan's attacks? Satan attacks with lies, and we defend ourselves by believing what God says, regardless of how Satan makes us feel. For example, let's say you are attacked with a feeling of fear. This is a common dart Satan uses. To defeat Satan you simply meet his lie with an affirmation of God's truth. "The Lord has not given me a spirit of fear, but of power and of love and of a sound mind" (see 2 Tim. 1:7).

Our emotions are often Satan's doorways into our minds. By faith we must stop him at the door. Regardless of what our emotions tell us, we must believe God. We may feel unworthy—it's a lie. We may feel rejected—it's a lie. We must renew our minds to the true knowledge of who we are (Col. 3:10). By faith we must accept what God says about us. For faith is our protection against Satan's lies.

The Helmet of Salvation

As we enter into warfare prayer, our armor must include the helmet of salvation. This means that we must have the Holy Spirit living inside of us (Eph. 6:18). The helmet covers and protects the mind. This is also the work of the Holy Spirit. We must live in the power and under the direction of the Holy Spirit. Fleshly power and reasoning are worthless in a spiritual conflict (2 Cor. 10:3-5). Therefore, we must submit our minds, wills, and emotions to the authority of God's Spirit (Gal. 5:16, 25).

The Sword of the Spirit

Lastly, our armor must include the sword of the Spirit— God's Word. Throughout this book we have noted the importance of Scripture in our prayers. The Bible is the anchor of our faith and the source of our authority.

But God's Word has another use in the context of spiritual warfare and warfare prayer. It is a weapon to be used against our adversary Satan. But this weapon won't do us any good if we don't know how to use it. We must direct the Word of God at Satan in a spiritual attack. There are specific Scriptures that deal with specific attacks of Satan. We are to saturate our prayers with these passages. In this way we can bind Satan from our lives and from the lives of others.

The Strategy of Warfare Prayer

Now that we better understand the preparation of the warfare prayer, let's turn our attention to the warring itself. How are we to deal with the enemy in our lives and in the lives of others? We have already said that the essence of spiritual warfare is binding and loosing (Matt. 16:19). But what are we to bind and loose? This question is answered in the following Scripture passage:

> For the weapons of our warfare are not carnal, but mighty through God to the pulling down of strongholds; casting down imaginations, and every high thing that exalteth itself against the knowledge of God, and bringing into captivity every thought to the obedience of Christ (2 Cor. 10:4-5).

We, through warfare prayer, have the responsibility and power to come against the strongholds Satan has in our lives and in others' lives.

Strongholds

A stronghold is an area of sin that has become part of our lifestyle. It may be a harmful habit (drugs, fornication, smoking) or it may be an attitude (rejection, loneliness, worry, doubt). We use a whole arsenal of rationalizations and speculations to support these habits or attitudes. But the knowledge on which these strongholds are based directly opposes God's truth (v. 5).

Satan pumps us full of lies which secure these strongholds. They may sound like this, "There's really nothing wrong with this music—I don't listen to the words anyway." Or, "I just drink a little when I get nervous." And haven't we all said, "The police won't pull me over for going 60 mph, so it's OK"?

Our responsibility as Christians is to tear down these strongholds through Spirit-filled prayers. How? There is only one weapon—the sword of the Spirit. We must fight these lies with God's Word. We must fight specific lies with specific truths.

A young woman continuously struggled to discipline her eating habits. She realized it was a stronghold in her life and she fought to overcome it. First she pinpointed the subconscious lies she had believed about her problem. She thought she studied better if she snacked. She also thought that every time she felt hungry she *had* to eat. And she told herself that eating helped her handle her emotions better. But all these things were lies from Satan to keep her in bondage.

She accepted God's account of her life as His child. She believed that she was "a new creature" and that her life was hidden with Christ in God (Col. 3:3). She accepted the fact that she was not under the dominion of her flesh and its drives (Gal. 5:24).

Then she took portions of Scripture, like these mentioned, and memorized them. Every time she was tempted to eat when she knew she really didn't need to, she met Satan's lies with God's Word. She was consistently victorious from then on.

In our lives we need only ask God in faith to tear a

stronghold down and He will do it. Then we must immediately renew that part of our minds with the true knowledge of God's Word (Rom. 12:2). If we don't, we will be subject to the same lies again and again.

For example, you have a stronghold of self-condemnation. That is, after you sin and ask God to forgive you, you don't *feel* forgiven. You mope around under a cloud of guilt till you feel a sufficient time has passed and your fellowship with the Father can be restored.

To find victory, you must ask God to tear down this stronghold. Name it out loud. Rebuke the lies that Satan has used against you and tell God that you now accept the truth of His Word. A good Scripture to claim would be Romans 8:1. Also study God's forgiveness in the Scriptures. This will focus your attention on the truth. Then as you meditate on the truth, your mind will respond in a positive way.

Warring for the Saints

This principle of overcoming strongholds can be applied as we pray for other saints as well. But at some point in time, others must take the responsibility of renewing their own minds—we cannot do it for them. We can pray that God will tear down a specific stronghold in their lives, and He will do it. But if they don't rebuke the lies that protected that stronghold, the stronghold will come back. For only application of the truth can stand against Satan's lies.

One evening I shared with my son that God had shown me a stronghold of fear in my life. He smiled and said that the Lord had revealed this problem in my life to him the week before. He had been praying that God would tear down this stronghold and show me my need to renew my mind to the truth in this area. We both went away with a new appreciation for the power of prayer and for God's willingness to tear down our strongholds if we will only let Him.

When we pray for others, we must persist until God reveals to them the truths concerning their strongholds. We must pray that God will convict them of their sins and guide them into the truth. We must claim Christ's promise: "Howbeit when He, the Spirit of truth, is come, He will guide you into all truth: for He shall not speak of Himself; but whatsoever He shall hear, that shall He speak: and He will show you things to come" (John 16:13). The key is to pray continually. This is why our little "bless him" prayers really do no good. We need *specific* truths to combat *specific* strongholds.

Strongholds and the Lost

The lost are also in bondage to strongholds. Strongholds such as procrastination, immorality, self-righteousness, and doubt keep people from experiencing the new life available in Christ. We must ask God to show us what the specific strongholds are. We can then, by the authority invested in us by God, ask God to convict people of their strongholds.

Satan uses lies to keep lost people lost and Christians in bondage. Only through prevailing prayer do we have the hope and freedom that Christ offers. We must bind the spirits of deceit and loose the ministering spirits of truth (Heb. 1:14). This type of prayer sets in motion God's power in such a way that the demons tremble.

Paul wrote, "We wrestle not against flesh and blood" (Eph. 6:12). It is time we quit struggling against flesh and blood and deal with the *real* enemy. We have only one weapon. It is not preaching, teaching, singing, or organizing; it is the Word of God brought against Satan's lies through prayer. Our prayers build the kingdom of God and destroy the kingdom of Satan. But where there is no prayer, there is no warfare. Where there is no warfare, there is no spiritual reality. Where there is no spiritual reality, there is no victory. Where there is no victory, there is nothing glorifying to God.

Christ said, "I glorified Thee on the earth, having accomplished the work which Thou hast given Me to do" (John 17:4, NASB). We, like Christ, are to glorify the Father. But if we don't enter into the warfare of prayer, we will never fulfill God's plan for our lives. If we don't pray, we serve no purpose in God's framework of eternity.